PRAISE FO

T0028621

"Can a book deflect predators? Is ... .ly
can take a new posture, training itself to become a gentleman,
an atmosphere, a counter-product, a galaxy? 'There is no limit to how
much you can learn about electricity' is one of the many sentences or
lines in *Dream Rooms* that both absorbed and emitted attention, the
strong and sometimes overwhelming energy that accompanies what
the writer calls emergence. 'Nothing alive belongs to anyone.' Yes."

—Bhanu Kapil

"A quick-witted, momentum-filled, tender rebellion of a book."

**—Chase Joynt, director of *Framing Agnes* and co-author of *You Only
Live Twice: Sex, Death and Transition***

"These pages are like the best conversations I have had with poets,
relentlessly pushing through the mystery together. There is no choice
but to learn a new way to hold what we think we know or drop
it on the ground. 'When you hurt one of us you hurt us all,'
writes River Halen in a book I would buy for you if I knew you,
driven to share this brilliant conversation."

—CAConrad, author of *AMANDA PARADISE: Resurrect Extinct Vibration*

"One of this book's many major achievements is its delightful continual
configuration of everyday objects (wearing fuzzy white socks so ailing
bunny feels at home; a broken razor leaving one very hairy leg shaved,
one not) into a procedural for unbounded being. A voice moves from
rental room to room, unspooling a life lived with divinely smudged or
entangled boundaries between human and animal, between friendship
and love, between prescribed and transitioning gender. *Dream Rooms*
is a marvellous confection of the author's definition of *revolution*—a
series of small, courageous, flawed attempts to risk everything."

—Gail Scott, author of *Permanent Revolution*

DREAM ROOMS

DREAM ROOMS

RIVER HALEN

ESSAIS SERIES NO. 15

Book*hug Press
Toronto 2022

Library and Archives Canada Cataloguing in Publication

Title: Dream rooms / River Halen.
Names: Halen, River, author.
Identifiers: Canadiana (print) 20220218935 | Canadiana (ebook) 2022021896X
ISBN 9781771667784 (softcover)
ISBN 9781771667791 (EPUB)
ISBN 9781771667807 (PDF)
Subjects: LCGFT: Essays. | LCGFT: Poetry. | LCGFT: Creative nonfiction.
Classification: LCC PS8615.A387 D74 2022 | DDC C814/.6—dc23

The production of this book was made possible through the generous assistance
of the Canada Council for the Arts and the Ontario Arts Council.
Book*hug Press also acknowledges the support of the Government of Canada
through the Canada Book Fund and the Government of Ontario
through the Ontario Book Publishing Tax Credit and the Ontario Book Fund.

Book*hug Press acknowledges that the land on which we operate is the traditional
territory of many nations, including the Mississaugas of the Credit, the Anishnabeg,
the Chippewa, the Haudenosaunee, and the Wendat peoples. We recognize the
enduring presence of many diverse First Nations, Inuit, and Métis peoples and are
grateful for the opportunity to meet, work, and learn on this territory.

The field was commotional: it did not allow stasis.
To enter it, you had to be in motion, and to see where
you were you had to be in motion, and not just moving
your body around constantly, frantically naming
stations, then moving at varying speeds between them,
but also naming with impermanence, seeing objects as
in the middle of some process, and understanding your
seeing as impermanent as well...

—Renee Gladman, *Calamities*

CONTENTS

SELF LOVE

I don't know if I was given
James Herriot books to read as a child
because I wanted to be a veterinarian
or if I wanted to be a veterinarian
because I was given James Herriot books
to read as a child. Each day at work
in all the books, James Herriot, a veterinarian
put his hand inside a cow's cunt
and then later I tried this in the tub.
It hurt but I didn't stop.
There were no women in my childhood
in books or real life
just men and cows—
the women I loved were all men
and the women I didn't, cows.
No women in this exploration, either
just a man and a cow
and I was both—I did not know
how profoundly—this hurt
sometimes I got curious
asked a strange man for a ride—
I mean my mom, of course—
to a farm with real livestock
I could interview, waving fistfuls of
young grass and clover through the fence
to soften the electric fact.
Sometimes a cow slipped
a key in the ignition
and drove me there
like heroines herded
through the Victorian era
to fall in love or maybe
into a profession.

SOME ANIMALS AND THEIR HOUSING SITUATIONS

Nov. 30, in the year the St. Helena Giant Earwig was declared extinct

I had expected the bunny to be enormous, but it turned out to be only the regular size. I had confused the kind it was—Holland Lop—for another kind—Flemish—when I was googling, I guess because Holland and Belgium are so close together, if you are thinking about distance from a certain perspective, as a rabbit probably wouldn't.

Flemish rabbits, also known as Flemish Giants, are the size of sheepdogs, fat children, but taller, longer when stretched out, and I imagined the bunny would lie next to me in bed like a softer, sweatless, riskier version of my ex, with a heart rate up to 325 beats per minute.

Dec. 7

The bunny's name is Frog.

For a week he hopped around the pale green apartment, demolishing lettuces in a beautiful, systematic way, and I watched him as an example of how to live. He was perfect at it. A glad little equation.

But today he stopped. First hopping, then eating. Now he no longer poos his gemlike droppings. Drool mats the fur along his jaw and throat, and makes a dark trail down to his shoulder.

I should clarify that Frog is not my bunny. What's mine are two sweaters, four T-shirts, a sports bra, eight pairs of slightly stretched-out underwear, a pair of jeans, a pair of too-tight beige cotton-polyester blend pants that I have not yet realized make me look naked from the waist down when I am seen from a distance, a raincoat, a staticky zip-up fleece jacket, black socks with holes in the toes, my favourite red woolly socks, and spongy white athletic socks with dirty bottoms.

Four rechargeable batteries and a charger and a dirty laptop and a charger and a vibrator and a charger and an ancient orange flip phone and a charger and a small electric blanket you don't charge just plug in for instant romance.

A vial of concealer and small squirt bottles of soap and shampoo and two tinted lip balms and some books and receipts and new and previously chewed gum and a rust-coloured reusable menstrual cup and a papier-mâché necklace I dropped in the toilet once and an empty, fraying black suitcase on wheels.

I had some money, too, but I spent it—almost all of it—on fixing up my ex's house, for reasons I guess could best be described as cultural.

It happened effortlessly. My ex is supposed to pay me back, and I mostly believe he will, but he hasn't yet.

We have disagreed about some things. The amount. Right now it's tense, like in the nineteenth century.

Not having my money gives me these melodramatic feelings. Or maybe they are just dramatic feelings. It depends on whether the feelings are only inside me or whether they are externally justified. If they are valid in the present or just historically. Anyway, I'm broke and homeless. That's the feeling.

Frog belongs to Soft Force, a young stranger with good posture who rented me his apartment at a discount this month in exchange for keeping Frog alive, and now Frog is dying. Soft is not wealthy, objectively, as far as I can tell, and I am not completely poor—others are far more broke and homeless, and I think about them increasingly, identifying a little (*what if, what if*) but mostly just wanting to hold them and not be them, as my ex held and did not want to be me, and I can't tell yet if this hypocrisy is the first step toward love or just the same old violent tantrum, a means or illusion of control—and no one knows for sure about Frog yet, but still everything is relative and I have these feelings.

Dec. 8

What belongs to Frog is a special threadbare towel that people use to wrap him up like a sausage.

The sausage goes in a cat carrier that normally belongs to the neighbour's cats. I apply my lip balm but forget the concealer, and we wait by the side of the road in the rain in these states of half-convincing disguise.

The cab driver tenses as I slide Frog in across the back seat.
"It's a bunny," I offer.
"Oh."

Frog's tension, which, because of his various casings as well as his status as a tiny animal, can only be known by inference, is different from the cab driver's, having to do with his body as opposed to possessions. Some cab drivers own their cabs. Others lease them. It feels important to consider whether this particular cab driver owns this particular cab, whether any of us in this situation is really free.

It occurs to me that I have no personal reason to be tense, but am present as a kind of bowl.

When we arrive at the clinic, the cab driver presses his palm into the seat cushion where Frog was, checking, I guess, for bunny piss, and there is something in the way his hand moves—suspicious and at the same time purely sensing—that makes me think of everything I don't know yet.

He took a shortcut to get us here, a route I didn't recognize, and it occurs to me while the vet is talking—she recommends exploratory surgery—that this city, where I used to live, very near where I grew up, is no longer mine. After the breakup I wanted to come back, to double-check. But to be honest I feel kind of lost here.

Nothing alive belongs to anyone. Everyone is constantly learning this and forgetting this, and learning this and forgetting this and learning.

Dec. 9

When I press the black lever, the kitchen light dims, and when the toast hops out, brightness.

I'm learning about electricity and I'm learning about Soft Force.

He has a liquor cart stocked with gin and an array of special glasses. It is dustless.

The real skulls of two animals, one a cow I think, with big friendly sockets, are mounted on the wall.

China plates and tiny framed pictures of men and dogs and an even coat of hospital-room green paint.

There is a steel mesh bookcase containing a number of books that look good to me, that maybe one day I'll read, as well as a bunch of books I am actively avoiding, plus two guides on how to be a gentleman.

I invite my sister over to get drunk on cheap red wine and learn to be a gentleman.

I pull some records from a low shelf just to see—*The Kick Inside* and *Pet Sounds*. It's okay to leave them on the floor because the bunny's not here right now.

Sex according to the guides is exactly what you'd expect.

Modern gentlemen should always wear the most expensive socks they can afford.

I always do! They are from the drugstore or Loblaw's or my birthday or, once, on an impulse, the Running Room. At any given moment, the vast majority of the world's population is impeccably gentlemanly in terms of socks.

Now we are rummaging in the closets. We find some drugs, no, herbs, no, natural cleaning products or something nasty-smelling to sprinkle on plants. The smell is a mystery. The mystery is Soft's.

Dear Soft, I am wearing my socks all over your floors and into your mushy bed sometimes at night because it's cold and I am lonely.

Wearing socks and tearing through your kitchen cabinets in search of food. Don't you have any food. Soft, I have just been dumped. By a man I lived with until he went crazy and stopped loving me. You'd have to be crazy not to love me. Wouldn't you? What the fuck is the deal with all this empty space plus a parcel of dried fish.

Soft, no, seriously. Where is your secret bulk section, your hint-of-lime chips.

Please, Soft, I'm begging you. Some heavily salted caramel kettle corn for my sister—she's done nothing wrong at all.

For fuck's sake, Soft.

If I stand on this chair.

If I kneel on your damp countertop in these cute athletic socks with dirty bottoms, like a real gentleman.

If seeing me on my knees like this would turn you on.

When I snoop inside your closets it's a kind of prayer. Your diary a holy book. Just because I can't locate your stack of vintage pornographic magazines does not mean you don't have one.

The Kick Inside, I am realizing, refers to fetuses. *Pet Sounds* is more obvious.

Dec. 11, in the year of the only remaining Rabb's Fringe-Limbed Tree Frog. He is male. The last known female died in 2009. He's held on awhile, though. Maybe he'll make it through another year.

When I pick Frog up from surgery his chin is shaved, which makes him look like an imaginary order of monk.

Rabbits' teeth grow continuously to sustain the continuous eating rabbits must do to live. What happened is they grew so long on one side they pierced the gums, which healed, and then were pierced again, and healed, and were pierced and healed at such rapid intervals the processes merged, so the more appropriate term might be *peeled* or *hearsed.*

Between the stitches, where they drained the abscess, are ugly gaps. At these I am to aim syringefuls of iodine three times a day. Sucked up from the bottle it is like cherry juice or dilute blood, a measured red quantity of jewel. Over time I expect it will turn Frog pink, since he is mostly white, and the process imprecise, like basting.

Other syringes, full of medicine, are to be aimed at Frog's mouth.

I chase Frog around all evening with the syringes. Near midnight he backflips out of my hands and thwacks his little horse skull on the edge of the glass coffee table. *Oh sweetheart.*

On the verge of Dec. 12

The internet suggests rabbits can be tricked into eating medicine if it's stirred into a fruit purée. I go to Shoppers Drug Mart and buy three kinds of baby food. It is midnight, but they are open, because Shoppers Drug Mart is a place like the human brain, always either awake or dreaming, processing something.

I've decided the clerk is handsome with his tired eyes and unusual skin texture. While I am reaching into my raincoat pocket for my credit card, an image bubbles up. The clerk wrapped in a towel, arms pinned to his sides, kind of mummified, struggling ineffectually. Meanwhile I'm pressing a syringe of baby food between his lips. *Heyyy sweetie*, I say in the thought. *Gorgeous, hold still.* His breath becoming all appley. Not a sex act per se, but one of those elliptical activities people sometimes still pay each other for. In this scenario who would pay whom?

And meanwhile he is thinking things too. He must think I've given birth. I have given birth to a baby and it's back at home, waiting for me to return to it with this miniature mushed-up orchard.

Frog loves baby food. I am pretty sure if he could choose, he would eat nothing but baby food. But it gives him diarrhea.

Dec. 13

The landlord is an old man I have not met yet, but who inquired about my character and the nature of my shoes (loud or quiet) before I came. Setting him aside, the living room is first Soft's, and then mine, but right now it is Frog's meadow.

In the meadow I squat surrounded by a smattering of bunny poop while Frog licks my bare legs or jeans devotedly. I tithe him a percentage of my cut-up apple and let him eat the edge of a rare book. I am far enough down the line to inherit Soft's possessions that I offer everything freely. I am not too fussed about the condition of the wooden couch legs or the album covers. I wear my white socks, which Frog seems to view as company. He gets really excited and starts to hop around between my feet, as if in a herd. The new purpose of my white socks is bunny lingerie. I suddenly feel so great in them. I worry I will step on Frog but I also want to prance.

In theory I have the power to do things Frog doesn't like, but in practice I don't. There is no way to be liked while squirting iodine into a wound, which is what is currently required.

I don't especially mind whether I make myself unlikeable to Soft, who has a giant painting of himself and his girlfriend in their swimsuits on the wall of his office that I practise the following conversation with:

—Hi, Soft.
—Hi.
—I know you have just spent a thousand dollars on your bunny, but you need to spend more.
—Why?

—Because it offends my sense of myself as a loveable person to continue to try to wrestle your bunny into inescapable holds when he does not want to be held. Also, it is exhausting, and no holds are inescapable, it turns out.

—If I were there I could totally show you some inescapable holds.

—I would rather you show me your credit card number.

Soft is mostly naked in the picture, which gives me an advantage.

Dec. 15

When I drop Frog off at the vet's the second time, he has to sit on the waiting-room floor in his cage while I fill out some forms and explain about the baby food. During that time he makes friends with a cat who is loose in the office. By "friends" I mean that Frog makes nibbley faces at the cat through the bars, and the cat marks Frog's cage all over with the scent gland at the corner of its mouth, possessively. They are about the same size; Frog is an old buck of ample girth, and the cat is petite, although a predator. Maybe this is the relationship model that will solve everything.

Dec. 17, in the year the last known Forest Skink, named "Gump," died in a zoo

Alice Notley says, "Don't alliterate or you'll go to hell." I am doing something far worse: walking around the apartment singing Tori Amos's "Playboy Mommy" with the bunny in mind.

You seemed ashamed
Ashamed that I was
A good friend of American soldiers

The use of the word "friend." What Tori means is most likely not love, but the performance of particular acts of care in exchange for something in a situation of precarity.

Also "soldier," synonymous here with "man."

All these little hooks in language holding a very big thought together like a net across the world.

Dec. 18

The bunny has been picked up from the vet's by a female friend of Soft's, _____, who works as a veterinary assistant and so knows how to flush out wounds. I have noticed that men are often surrounded by a constellation of helpful women with different skill sets. Do they collect them consciously, I wonder.

Frog's vet is a young woman, and all of her assistants are young women. All of the women involved in flushing out Frog's wound perform a carefully choreographed series of trade-offs and competent hand motions that spell a gently glowing suggestion in the night sky.

Soft's apartment was very tidy when I moved in, with all the objects put away in places far from where they are needed (the toaster in a cabinet, the toothbrushes behind a mirror, the dish rack below the sink, the bunny's cage in a corner of the office). I have moved all of the objects to exactly where they are needed. The bunny, although not here right now, lives in the centre of the living-room floor.

Dec. 20, in the year the Quiver Tree was unable to grow or disperse quickly enough

Living in another person's home is like wearing their atmospheric outfit over time. I feel these little gusts. My body slips into position. So this is what it's like. Or is it.

My clothes are all wrong for me. But Soft's are even more wrong— huge. Like for a different species.

Then Gillian bikes over in her cycling shoes with clips on the bottom. She doesn't have anything good to walk in. Don't worry, I say, and dig out a pair of Soft's leather boots. I know exactly where he keeps them. They are just like my boots, but three times bigger. Gillian looks like she's in a fairy tale as we stroll up the road to get lunch.

When my soup comes, I mention that I might start calling myself a lesbian, to see if the word changes anything. I'll probably still just fuck whoever, as usual, I hedge. But I would like to give the women a promotion.

Gillian agrees. She still loves men. For some reason I worry that if I'm not careful I might ruin this for her. I'm a very persuasive speaker.

Gillian's feet are so big right now I can't stop looking. Do they feel big, I wonder. On the inside.

Dec. 21

On the counter is a jar of puréed carrots with a picture of a baby's head on it. Yesterday I was almost lazy enough to eat the contents instead of buying food. Today it's here as incriminating evidence when the landlord appears at the kitchen window, suddenly as an animal, and raps his small, wild fist on it.

Pets are not allowed in the apartment, and luckily, none are here.

I'm at the table in the living room, sitting in my sweaty nightshirt, braless as a real live nymph or cow, very visible. "Hello," I say over my shoulder, wishing my head could swivel all the way around, like an owl's.

Dec. 23

Now here is a bunny, carried out to my mom's car by _____, who is covered in a gentle down of stray hairs of many different colours, and whose sweatpants have been perforated, as if by an adoring wolf pack, to a kind of coarse lace.

I'm spending Christmas with my mom in the suburbs, and Frog comes as my date. The drive is long in rabbit-time. When we arrive, my mom serves carrots, apple pieces wrapped in kale (almost like sushi), and a grape. Three grapes. Frog eats everything while we watch, hungry to see him satisfied, and it does not take long before he gets spectacularly sick, his diarrhea leaking all over my mom's pale carpets, all over the ancient towels we lay down over them.

Frog licks his paws and moves them in circles, grooming, until the whole of him is an evenly mottled shitty grey-brown. My sister spends the evening sitting beside him with a damp washcloth, attempting to undo a particular matted clump on his forehead we refer to as his "poonicorn horn." My mom buffs him dry with a Kleenex. He is so loved, and he has never looked worse. I make him hay salad to calm his stomach. Hay salad is hay snipped into tiny pieces with celery leaves and shredded kale mixed in as an incentive. It drifts on the carpet until the room seems more like a mown field.

Frog with his luxurious, soft, streaked coat, that is heaven to run my fingers through even now, is the literal aftermath of one of those toilet paper commercials featuring a fluffy white creature people are meant to desire, subliminally—or kind of blatantly, actually—to rub against their assholes.

Dec. 27

Frog's ears never go above half mast, but they spend a lot of time there, sticking straight out like a propeller when he grooms.

Frog's ass is as flat as a frying pan from, I guess, so much sitting on it.

Of earth, water, air, fire, Frog's element is earth, but not all of it. Carpet is a type of earth. Tile and linoleum and polished wood are earth. Of these, only carpet is inhabitable.

What happens when Frog finds himself on tile: panicked pawing-kicking as if he might drown.

I do not know what Frog would do in water.

Dec. 28

My ex had clinical anxiety. This fact does not explain everything. But some parts of our relationship were a tile to him.

Today I take the three towels that are in Soft's closet and lay them down in the tiled hallway, which connects to the carpeted office and bedroom. The way dreams connect to new landscapes that are really just the same familiar landscapes. Frog begins to race along the towels and into each room and back again, into each room and back again, growing increasingly excited.

Eventually Frog gets to the bathroom. He pauses, craning his neck out over the cool, ocean-blue ceramic floor with my stray hairs scattered over it like drawn-on waves. He twitches there a moment. Then he jumps.

If a man is someone you do things for, then a panicked man is not less of a man but more of one.

Dec. 29, in the year there were five remaining Northern White Rhinos

My sister comes over again. She's fascinated by the giant swimsuit painting. Who wouldn't be. She discovers a date on it, and it suggests that the woman in it could not possibly be Soft's current girlfriend, but has to be his ex.

Then she finds a signature. The painting of Soft in his swimsuit turns out to be not of Soft at all, nor of any of his girlfriends, barring a huge coincidence, but a poorly executed early work of an artist who has since become talented and famous.

I had thought Soft was keeping the ugly painting out of love, or possibly vanity, but maybe it's more like an investment.

As to the question of why Soft bears such resemblance to the young man in the painting:
- a) Soft was drawn to the painting because he saw himself in it;
- b) I see Soft in the painting because Soft is everywhere around me;
- c) All young men are Soft.

Dec. 30

Soft's kitchen is not the full size a kitchen longs to be. I spend a lot of my time in it swearing. Everything is put away in neat interlocking stacks that do not like to be disturbed. Frog is either used to the sound of sudden crashes, or he is deaf, or he hears on a different frequency altogether. Or for him the kitchen is an unreal place whose events are mythological and therefore not frightening.

Kitchens are traditionally feminine spaces that women have longed to either escape or upgrade the cabinetry in. But Frog wants nothing so desperately as to get in. I extend his towel-road as far as the cabinet below the sink, so we can keep each other company while I stand aimlessly, not cooking.

Frog hops to the end of his road and sits facing the fridge. He spring-loads his hind legs and waits, I assume, for the white door to open.

Frog is too fragile, tiny, and edible to ever do his share of meal preparation, but I don't begrudge him this fact. Nor his suicidal determination. The absurdity of our situation is a product of culture.

Dec. 31

In my dream it sounds like someone put their running shoes in the dryer. *Thunk-thunk-thunk-thunk*. No, someone is jiggling my doorknob. He is persistent. Could it be the landlord.

I haul myself upright. It's 5 a.m. There is no one. I walk out to the living room. Frog is lying twisted on the floor of his cage, kicking his legs out behind him, trying to stand up. Feet thumping percussively against the food dish. His efforts have carved deep circles in the bedding.

It's too early to do anything, and too late, but I know it is my role to remain in denial about *too late* until the very end. I sit listening because it's hard to watch. *Thunk-thunk-thunk*. At seven I call Soft, then the vet. Then I shower, circling my palms up under my armpits repetitively.

When I emerge, Frog is lying in an elegant tangle like a stained white scarf, half covered in hay. I feel around for a heartbeat anyway.

Jan. 1, in the year after Plectostoma sciaphilum, a species of snail that lived on a single hill in Malaysia, was wiped out by a cement company

I have this feeling like I hosted a party and it went really wrong. Everyone went home early or died.

Tori Amos knows my feeling. "Don't judge me so hard, little girl, so you got a playboy mommy," she sings to her miscarried baby.

As if dying is just another snarky thing that people do to one another, that *women* do to one another, passing judgment for bad hostessing.

In the Christian myth of creation, Force invents mortality as a punishment. The behaviour to be punished is Eve's. Either (a) she serves Adam substandard food, or (b) in the story, substandard food symbolizes sex, which Eve initiates. The moment where death first becomes a possibility is also the beginning of shame.

Tori is ashamed. And in Tori's description the dead baby is ashamed too, of Tori. Everyone in the song is ashamed except possibly the American soldiers, whose feelings are not described.

Soft's diary, which I am not proud to have read, but which I cannot deny knowledge of, is mostly an account of services provided to him. Sandwiches and how good they were. Lobster rolls. Blow jobs. Concerts. People who gave him rides or painted his apartment for him. His feelings are not described. It's an incredible document. I wish that I could publish it. I think that it would captivate its audience, who would intuitively understand that for a certain kind of young man with a certain amount of money—a man who is not and never will be an American soldier, but who at the same time completely *is*—these transactions are indistinguishable from life itself. The diary is life itself.

later

Victim Index
1. The rest of the world
2. Rabbits in fiction
3. Frog
4. Dead babies
5. American soldiers
6. My ex
7. Me
8. My ex
9. Soft Force? (Except I read his diary, so I guess he should come before me)
10. The vet
11. The landlord
12. American soldiers
13. Soft Force? (If I put him here he's God)
14. This list is endless and loops back on itself, like the universe.

& later

I am lying on my back, humming my vibrator down past my navel and into my thicket. It is the kind with two heads, one longer (for stimulating the G-spot) and one shorter (for stimulating the clitoris), that people refer to as a Rabbit, though mine is a knock-off and so is technically called something else. I have forgotten the name.

I am trying to masturbate in a lesbian way. I'm unfocused. Pick a woman, I tell myself. Anyone. Think of her. But my feelings make a kind of constellation.

In the galaxy there are stars enough that when a rabbit dies you can find its outline in the sky, even if the rabbit is a hunchback or has its legs sticking out at a broken angle.

The galaxy hums when you turn it on, like a machine, and rabbits can breed and die and be born again as often as necessary. Some live their whole lives in captivity.

Rabbits are related to horses in a distant way that rabbits would never think about, or maybe they do.

The galaxy is outside me, and inside too.

Horses can bolt like lightning.

But when the stars run out of batteries, I plug them in.

A rabbit is the softest thing to rub against.

My relationship with my ex was an open one. I am thinking of someone I fucked a little sometimes, with permission. But permission is a room that no longer exists. Where is that person now?

The toast *pop-pops* like a firework until the night sky is lit.

There is no limit to how much you can learn about electricity.

Jan. 2

Do I want the rabbit cremated, asks the vet.

It's not my decision, I say, and text Soft. His number's always right on top these days.

In the children's story *The Velveteen Rabbit*, a toy bunny is sentenced to be burned after coming into contact with a human child's scarlet fever. Because desire as funnelled through the narratives of our culture burns all the lesser creatures.

When I was small, my dad taught me how to build a fire. He said the most effective method is to pile the wood exactly like a house, and I have remembered this. I am good at fire.

For a bonfire, pile the wood like a mansion.

The word bonfire has the word *bone* in it. It does not mean a good fire, from the French. It means a fire intense enough to burn bones.

later

I have this feeling that I died just now, of neglect. I mean of caring
very hard within a structure beyond my control. Anyway, I would
like to register my death as a protest. Not just against the ones
immediately above me, but at the highest level.

Jan. 3

The year in review:

Aphanius saourensis, eaten by introduced Gambusia fish

Bermuda Hawk (*Bermuteo avivorus*), "discovered" then declared extinct

Bermuda Night-heron (*Nyctanassa carcinocatactes*), "discovered" then declared extinct

Polar bears, increasingly resorting to eating goose eggs

Oceanic Parrot (*Eclectus infectus*), "discovered" then declared extinct

Rodrigues Blue-pigeon (*Alectroenas payandeei*), "discovered" then declared extinct

The only remaining Oahu Tree Snail, in captivity since 2011

Bermuda Flicker (*Colaptes oceanicus*), "discovered" then declared extinct

Christmas Sandpiper (*Prosobonia cancellata*), "discovered" then declared extinct

Acropora cervicornis and coral in general, in decline almost everywhere

Adélie penguins, less and less successful at breeding and raising young

North Island Snipe (*Coenocorypha barrierensis*), "discovered" then declared extinct

Finsch's Duck (*Chenonetta finschi*), "discovered" then declared extinct

Hodgen's Waterhen (*Tribonyx hodgenorum*), "discovered" then declared extinct

Howell's Spectacular Thelypody (*Thelypodium howellii ssp. spectabilis*), only five populations remaining

Saolas, lately so rare they are referred to as unicorns

February

Soft sends me a card at my next sublet, where I live with a fat black cat who moans a lot.

The front of the card says, "You're the bee's knees," in an attractive letterpress font, and I think about what that phrase means. I am the hinge in the leg of a tiny animal, that lives in huge communities, on which we all depend to make plants fruit and seed.

"You did not sign up for a sick bunny (and it was the last thing I expected!)" Soft has written inside. Also, "You did your very best for him." I want this to be true. I am in a state where I want truth in everything.

REASON

When I go to the bathroom
to cry about your failures
I do it just like you
if you were me
watching the mirror
to see if sympathy is possible
then trying my best
to cry more beautifully.
When two people are in a room like this together
that's a couple. They are rinsing
the come off, soaping their strap-on
towelling the temperature down
their legs, along their arms
it's called flossing
and when there are three
that's an accident
of a kind I've hoped for
and guarded against
since I was small.
My family did not keep
books in a magazine
rack by the toilet
they just sat
with the light of civilization
bleeding under the door
and luckily whenever
I got scared I just
bled instead
like magic into the bowl
and to this day if I
turn around three times
two hands will reach out
from the mirror's lemoned silver

and steal my face—
there is nothing stopping this—
a ghost will appear in the silver
with my face
said my friend
who was a child with me
on some tiles that
still exist as a pattern
in linoleum
and I did not tell anyone
I am still in love with her
and you don't have to tell me
you are now too
because feelings plus time
are public property
or they just die
in the art gallery in the middle of the day
I used the men's for sex
leapt up silently on the seat
when the attendant came in to touch
his hair, a camera was installed
above a bald eagle's nest
to stream their hatching
love and casual
cruelty to my face
which was gripped
by an ordinary feeling:
I like looking at them
looking like me so much
there is a room just for
being and looking
for eagles
it's the whole outdoors
and I keep reading
it will be ending soon

but I can't seem to cry about it
beautifully enough
you know they shit
into clean running water too
whenever it's an option
I leave the door open
for some reason
I want my crying to carry.

ALL THE PARTS, MOVING

There is no such thing as literature.
Everything is just a diary
or a manifesto
I said at the table while chewing.
I was trying to be like those men in movies
who talk about ideas while the women bring little plates
of tapenade and torn loaves
except I was alone
that's how I think best
and I don't believe ideas and loaves
move independently.

Alone has to do with becoming
bodyless
it isn't possible
anyway mirrorless
the reason I can't think in coffee shops
those publics
that aren't publics
which are everywhere.
It has to do with bathing
in an eyeless air
until an argument, me-shaped
rests its elbow on a surface
like my thigh.

A diary is a record of life as it happened
leading to feelings in the present.
A manifesto is feelings in the present
leading to life as it is dreamed
for the diaries of the future.
The notion that there is some place outside
unrelated to feelings about the past

or the future as dreamed by a physical head
of a certain weight on a spine
is just religious.

As for poetry, let's consider something aesthetically
complete, like chewing gum hardening
in a little pink or white wad with tooth marks in it
on a sidewalk where someone spat it out.
The tooth marks come from adult
molars which are a conversation between childhood
food and fairies and belief in
parental income and bristly
petrochemicals and the gold-tipped tools
of the professions.

Chewing is what practically everyone has to do
to live. An early lover used to tell me
"Enough with the dentistry"
meaning stop wedging my tongue into that place
above the gumline during make-outs.
I was exploring destiny.

The people who spit after they chew right there in public
are not brave, they have permission
except for the ones who do not have permission:
They are brave.

SIX BOXES

One day, finally, after several years of numbtime, and a lifetime before that, when the details were not yet known to me, I went to my shelf and made the section. As I singled out each spine and moved it to the space I'd cleared below, I pictured the blurbs and jacket copy replaced by short, true summaries of violence: *This man beat and bruised women writers without consent during sex. This man attempted to kill his collaborator, a woman writer. This man encouraged his women writing students to drink to the point of passing out; some now believe, but cannot be sure, they were assaulted. This man groped women writers at parties. This man sent a death threat to his ex, a woman writer. This man saddled his ex, a woman writer, with an enormous debt. This man, without warning, shoved his tongue sequentially into the mouths of two women writers who happened to be sitting on either side of him. This man tried to coerce a woman writer into sex by withholding a reference letter at the last minute. This man repeatedly dated his women writing students and assaulted some. This man addressed a woman writer on a ferry deck. He told her he would push her off, then lunged at her, turned, and walked away.*

In the way that books all together on a shelf are repetitious—colour, format, author names, paper texture, smell, themes, font, images, letters, words—these acts circled back on themselves. As I made the section I began to access a feeling of vertigo, the way I think you are supposed to feel when you read about Borges's infinite library. People, people, words and people, all of nature, sounds, syllables, the alphabet recombining: Many things on the list had been done by more than one man. Some of the men were the same man. These were just the men I knew about, the books I happened to own. I had been social with all of them. There were more acts than I yet knew about, and more men than I could ever be friendly with or successfully ignore, and some acts committed by people who weren't men, and many people who had written books.

Hello, Literature, I said, addressing it directly for the first time. This love I'd had since childhood. Because the occasion of my standing there, in the lamplight with the scuffed white Ikea unit and the growing pile of pulled volumes, was love, just as the occasion of my purchases and attention and friendships and conversation and education and paid and unpaid work commitments and relationships and gifts and time alone with words in bed had been love. People are social creatures. The occasion of everything—however indirectly—is love.

*

There was the conversation I had with S about the section. S had been feeling what I had been feeling, and had made a section too, and had put the section in boxes, two of them, and was going to have a book burning. I was in awe of this decision.

She had given it a lot of thought and had arrived at a place of clarity: Thrift shops—not an option. Then other people would buy the books, ignorant of the violence they meant. The street—same. You would not leave a loaded gun in a box by the road. Recycling—a possibility. But the glue in the bindings apparently fucks up the municipal process.

At the same time I felt, acutely, that I could not do this with my own section, not yet. I still had questions.

Here were the words of the rapists and manipulators and assailants written down. If I studied very carefully, maybe I could identify the warning signs, learn to spot danger in an aesthetic, in a grammar.

I didn't see the violence because (a) I did not read the book, or (b) I did not see the violence in the book, or (c) the violence was invisible in the book, and then later or beforehand or all along it happened.

Or (d) I saw the violence in the book and everywhere in the world and didn't mind.

Seeing is a skill. Code-breaking is a skill. Minding is a skill. Total rage is a skill. I could keep these books in the closet like dumbbells in escalating stacks, for resistance training.

Was there a system by which I could identify the violence in other books, by authors I did not personally know. Was there a system I could master to NEVER ACQUIRE ANOTHER VIOLENT BOOK.

If I read the violent books I had loved backward, could I journey back inside myself and extract what I had eaten.

Was there a system of reading and writing and shelving that would lead to justice. I wanted to know.

Was I interested in justice or was I just having trouble letting go.

In the end S did not burn her books either. Blue bin, blue bin, blue bin.

*

Then I entered the part of my life where I was living beside a known monster, that I had chosen, that people judged me for.

My books took up a whole wall. It was unreasonable to try to hide them.

And I had cultivated the kind of life where it was normal for people to come over to drink and eat and smoke pot and develop feelings about my books, and by extension, me.

It was normal for me to talk about my feelings about my books, or even more normal to talk about something else, with my feelings about my books on display in the background.

As a young, feminine-looking, out bisexual person whose tastes were regularly questioned by guy friends, straight friends, lesbian friends, I had developed some defences against shame. I would feel it begin to well up inside me, and then I would do these little internal curl-ups to keep it down. I was strong. I was reasonably, adequately strong to be living in my particular body.

But now I encountered a different situation. The people judging me were not misguided or uninformed. They knew what I knew: My bookshelf was not a sanctuary or a clear idea or the beginning of an evolution in a positive direction. It was not a worthy love. It was a history of things I had let into my life that had not, for whatever reason, disappeared yet.

By this definition it was my body.

I wanted to tell people that I knew how bad my books were, that I was keeping the works of the rapists, the attempted murderers, especially, to learn from. That there was something about literature and my relationship to it I still had to figure out. This always seemed to come out wrong.

*

Most people I know have been raped. When it happened to me it wasn't by an author.

It started in a movie theatre, a full one. A friend—my supervisor at work—was sitting two rows ahead. When my rapist, sitting next to me, put his hand up my skirt and started shoving his fingers inside me, all at once, without warning, all I could think was *If my supervisor notices I'll get fired.* My efforts to get him to stop did not succeed. People began to stare.

I grabbed his wrist hard and stood up, and this got his hand out of me. He stood up too, and, as we fumbled to the end of the aisle, tried to put his hand back in. I held it away from me with both hands thinking *I can make this look like hand-holding.*

I took him home to my basement apartment. That seemed, in the moment, safer. On the way there, to keep his hand out of me, I ran. He ran too. For a while I was ahead. When he caught up with me, I went back to hand-holding, and we jogged alongside each other in a strange sort of arm wrestle. Google Maps now tells me the distance was thirteen blocks. Did he think this was romantic?

When we got inside, I said okay fuck me. I felt clear and on fire and insane in a way that was almost like having power. I felt like I had power. He did not fuck me. He took his limp dick out and slapped it across my face awhile. Slapped it against different parts of my body. Observing a little claw mark on my shoulder from when I'd had sex with a partner some days before, he called me a slut. Did he really say it so baldly. I remember the feeling. Then he zipped up his pants and I probably offered him tea or a drink and he either accepted or didn't then left. He complimented me on my books. At no point did I worry about the fact that I'd just shown a rapist, a stranger, where I lived. Safety as I understood it was not about avoiding physical harm but avoiding its amplification by witnesses.

I couldn't tell whether those people in the theatre were judging me or whether they were concerned for my well-being. If they were concerned for my well-being, it was not a feeling that led them to any particular action.

I know that there are people who would say, *Well what about your actions*. But I knew, even at the time, that I had aced this. *I aced this.*

I aced it so well I never really became a victim until nine years later, when my ex—the one from before I lived with the rabbit, and with whom I'd become friendly again—asked me directly: Have you ever been raped? and I had to admit it—I had to realize it, then admit it. It was a safe place to do so. I felt dizzy with the scale of my achievement: the bravery of my body, and the care my body had shown me in keeping this information tightly boxed until we arrived in a safe harbour. And now my mind shaking the contents loose and turning them instantly into conversation. I was having such a beautiful conversation. But at the same time I was disturbed to understand, in a way that would take time to sink in fully, that I had left my body and its political position just sitting there, somewhere outside myself, for nearly a decade of my life.

This was a decade in which I finished school and wrote a manuscript and mostly did not get fired from my jobs and became a published author. This was a decade in which I read and acquired a lot of books.

*

I visited a friend in another city. His girlfriend was moving in, and they were arranging their books on his shelf. She was hesitant about combining their books. He was enthused. Their books got very mixed up. Between the two of them, they owned many things I aspired to read. At one point in the afternoon, my friend picked a large hardcover up off the floor, Frederick Seidel's collected poems, and said, "I should get rid of this."

I knew what he meant because I owned this book too. In the beginning, it gave me pleasure—a kind of intellectual/sexual/ political/electrical excitement—but for the last several years it had sat undisturbed on my shelf in its alphabetical position, in a cloud of difficult emotions that manifested as dust along the tops of its pages. Other books I owned were dusty too, but the dust on this book was meaningful.

What had appealed to me about Frederick Seidel's poems was their "honesty." Frederick Seidel is an elderly white man with about twenty-two million dollars of wealth. In his poetry he describes in plain terms and without guilt all the different violent acts he is constantly committing. These encompass sexual violence, racist violence, economic imperialism, environmental destruction—everything. If the code of the privileged is not to speak about the harm they cause—to pretend ignorance—Frederick Seidel's poetry breaks this code. Or he is so privileged he never had to be aware of codes. Either way.

The other aspect of Seidel's poems that intrigued me was how ugly they were, aesthetically. The rhymes are clunky and excessive. The vocabulary is limited and repetitive, or it's various and unexpected but everything is a metaphor for "my dick." It is clear that he either does not care what anyone thinks about the beauty or sophistication of his poems or he enjoys the particular flex of being so powerful that he can compel people to find beauty and sophistication in anything he says.

Sometimes people referred to Frederick Seidel's work as satire. This never made sense to me. Are facts satire? Is documentary satire? Here was a straight-up account of the system I lived in from the psychopath in charge. Nobody had put him on trial but he was testifying anyway. I listened.

And then at a certain point I noticed the testimony was dragging on. It wasn't a trial, just a psychopath rambling on to me in the privacy of my apartment. This could go on indefinitely.

I began to think more about honesty.

There was a concept I was hungry for, that was articulated to me around this time in an essay by Ariana Reines, that "writing can be more than good." She proposes this, I believe, in part to guard against her own work being automatically dismissed for things like typos and a history of doing sex work to feed her unhoused mom, which she talks about in the essay. I thought about this idea in relation to Frederick Seidel's bad writing, which came from a position of enormous power. There was a fantasy I was indulging, maybe, the fantasy of having immunity to just speak.

If you had immunity to just speak, did your honesty even matter?

*

The same afternoon: I tell my friend that I think he should keep the book. I tell him he *has* to.

My friend is taken aback. I begin to explain. The course of action I am defending does not make sense, and therefore cannot be supported by a coherent argument, only fragments of ideas that I have heard or read or invented, interspersed with anecdotes and emotions.

When you have eaten a drug, if it is an official drug with packaging, you should keep the packaging. If it turns out you are poisoned, people will know what from. If you are eating a plant from the forest, keep one of its leaves.

When you have made a mistake, like confusing violence for honesty, you should not erase the record of that mistake until you have set it right. Setting literature right will take possibly forever.

I remember once when my friend and I were younger, and he spent the night in my cheap bachelor apartment. We stayed up, listening to music and falling asleep, but not really, him on the tiny floor space and me in the bed, and he looked at my bookshelf, which had fewer things on it then, and was probably not the same shelf, and he teased me for owning a book by a woman poet I was interested in, whose work he said was terrible.

I believed him. I kept the book and my shame about it for years, until my shame dissolved and the book didn't. The writing in it offered a different angle of testimony—abuse from the perspective of the survivor. I ask my friend if he remembers this. He doesn't. He is genuinely sorry and ashamed. It is hard for him to imagine ever not having been interested in this woman poet.

I remember a phase in my life after my friend made his remark when I listened attentively to what men thought I should read. The collected poems of Frederick Seidel was one of the books men recommended. I bought it with my own money.

I like my friend deeply, and I would like for him to have an experience of keeping a book he is ashamed of.

I remember a time when another friend of mine lived for a year without adding to the landfill. It was difficult. She bought food only in bulk—in cloth bags or glass containers for wet things—and refused to acquire any item not intended to either last forever or biodegrade. She failed a little, because at one point she broke a plate and decided not to keep the pieces. But otherwise she succeeded.

Not adding to the landfill can mean not creating any garbage, not bringing any home, or not being the one to throw it out. The lines between these accomplishments are not always clear. Some people live their whole lives without adding to the landfill, and we call this hoarding. Some people spend their whole careers in the humble occupation of garbage collector. I want my friend to think about this with me.

Compulsive hoarding can be the result of trauma, says the Wikipedia entry on compulsive hoarding. Trauma is very commonly the result of huge structural forces like racism, patriarchy, capitalism, the state. I can't get rid of the book because—I am just now putting this together—it has a relationship to my injuries.

And for my friend to get rid of the book while I keep it in shame would be unfair.

I do not tell my friend I am angry at him. I am angry because in the past I listened to him too much, and as a result experienced shame when I should not have, and gravitated toward interests I now find shameful. What is the definition of *friend*?

I have to admit that the night my friend teased me about the woman poet, I wanted to fuck him but wasn't brave enough. Years later, the night before this afternoon of book-sorting, I was brave enough. Having such a long delay between an idea and the corresponding action made me feel out of sync with my life, like complicated music.

I know what you are thinking, but I'm not angry about the fucking. It was friendly and bold, joyful. It was not shameful or cheating. It was an idea I had, and then it happened.

To get rid of a friend who is alive and changing because of a book I am struggling to throw out seems simultaneously very tempting and less than reasonable. "Bibliomania is a disorder involving the collecting or hoarding of books to the point where social relations or health are damaged," says the Wikipedia entry on compulsive hoarding.

It is probable I need to discard a lot of what I've known and loved.

*

There was a paralyzing moment after my friend and I slept together when I proposed, or he proposed, I forget exactly who proposed, that we should have a threesome with his girlfriend. If my interest in my friend was by that point mostly historical, my interest in his girlfriend was more current. The real electricity was a crush I had—a big one, just beginning to unfurl like some springtime thing—on a different woman. I felt swept up in its energy. I couldn't face it yet. So instead of finding a different place to stay I kept on being there one more night, and his girlfriend came home from her travels, and I gave them space to talk and tried to be exactly the right amount flirty and open and filthy and rained-on and approachable, and she took me grocery shopping and cooked everyone dinner, and I waited, like a scroll in a vault, to be chosen.

The three of us ate on the balcony in leafy air. Our knees touched. It was delicious. The table was so tiny. Some books spilled from the top of a stack to the floor with slapping sounds. I waited to see if I should make a move. Were there actions in this circumstance that were possible. But if so, they were invisible to me, and I didn't take any, and in the end I wasn't chosen.

The next day, I went home on the train. Before I went through my bookshelf and gutted it—and to be clear, I *gutted* it: five boxes into the recycling and six to the second-hand store, where I made the most money I had ever made that way, because violent books have a high resale value; I am sorry if I gummed up the system—I spent five or six months waiting. I was interested in the relationship between myself and my surroundings. I was interested in power: what knowledge is. I was interested in who it belongs to when I have it. I was alone with my body and I was contemplating boxes. How the empty ones are more useful if what you want to do is move. The heart is not infinite. Mine was once again becoming blank.

MIRROR

I believe the performer when she says her dance will involve doing
only those acts that bring her pleasure. I guess I'm more interested in
how pleasure might look than in all the ways there are to trick me.

She is wearing yellow shorts—the loose athletic ones that are, I think,
associated with masculinity but look almost exactly like a skirt. She is
wearing them over black tights.

There's a bit of yoga, then she takes her shoes off. That's interesting
about the shoes—I mean, to think about pleasure as the removal of
constraint. You could spend your whole life in that step, Phase One,
just thinking in the negative: bye, pinching.

Now it's a kind of crawling-listening. Spider hands and an ear against
the floor. Clicking of nails on lino or whatever the tiles are made of.
People don't think about tiles enough—these repeating patterns we're
always contacting, so similar from building to building, modulating
over time. Tiles made the rabbit panic, but this dancer seems curious.
What if we all looked at the floor all the time?

Admittedly, the way she's hunching doesn't look like fun. But pleasure
is a job sometimes. You have to process all the shit that's been
happening in your joints. You have to learn the range of possible
sounds your fingernails can produce. If you don't know the range,
what's the point in having preferences?

Now I'm thinking about my own body in the uncomfortable folding
chair. I can't help it. I uncross my legs. I'm part of the dance too.

All of us in folding chairs are exerting an unhelpful collective gravity.
The dancer could do anything, begin anywhere except for the gaze
of a bunch of people looking at her from the perspective of being

uncomfortable. It's limiting. At some point the dancer, if she's serious, will say goodbye to me. I'm ready for it.

OK, OK, we're approaching a climactic moment. She's taken out a jar of strong-smelling lotion and is rubbing it into her hands, the only skin besides her face currently exposed. I feel like this would be a more satisfying climax for her if she were wearing less—the lotion could hydrate more skin, bringing more pleasure—but of course it might not be a pleasure to her to be wearing less in front of an audience.

This is a dance about existing in a situation. The kind of situation that encourages your pleasures to be more austere.

The lotion has given its smell to the room—it's some kind of fresh spring floral muscle relaxant. Now pleasure is looking like a tough warrior stance taking up firm space with arms and legs, bending the knees and elbows defensively.

I uncross my legs.

You know what's kind of funny about the way she's holding her hands right now—it's a lot like the way I hold a pencil. My fingers are hypermobile, so to handwrite I have to overlap them, make my hand like a bird claw.

OK, OK, we seem to be moving into bedroom mirror mode. She turns some music on. Dance like nobody's watching. At my high school we had an unlikely tradition. It was an annual drag competition for graduating boys. The winner got a crown and had to come back the next year to lip sync a song, "The Duke of Earl." My high school at that time was not a place where it was safe for anyone to be out as queer, or for anyone to admit that an event like this one was extremely queer. Still, the competition existed. A lot of athletes joined. They would practise, alone in their bedrooms or in groups in someone's living room, how to dance in a skirt the way the performer is dancing in yellow athletic shorts.

I uncross my legs.

When everyone is watching, you have to be creative—ingenious— about creating a sense of safety around your pleasure.

She's lying on the floor now, on her side, in a pose I recognize from a different part of high school. A girl I had a crush on had read in a magazine about how to get the "best curve." You lie on one side with your legs kind of wrapped to accentuate the hip. Voilà: the "best curve." She would practise this. What can you do with the best curve? We didn't really know. We thought it might come in handy one day for something to do with sex.

Some clothes are coming off now. No more tights—thank god! No more curve, either. The music has been turned off. Child's pose. Total hiding of the face.

It's a series of advances and retreats—taking up space, expanding in your body, then retreating from that expansion which was never really encouraged and so caused a new set of problems.

Hiding is OK. It's OK.

I uncross my legs.

HONEYMOON

So there was never any pure time
if pure time exists for anyone, I do not know
I think of when you gave me
my pet name after
you came so hard that afternoon
on the rented bed
the month or so when you would say things like
"Oooh, you like taking your credit card out
in front of your friends, Power?"
if I tried to pay or
"Some sugar in your coffee, Power?"
if I tried to sip or
"Aww, Power—your head hurting you again?"
if I touched my temple
even or especially in public
and I would blush as if I really were
a public utility
lighting up information
for others to read
we were on a trip
the purpose of which was
getting a copper birth control device
extracted from my cervix
without paying a lot of money
in interprovincial medical fees
I was moved
that you came too
I remember when I got the IUD
I thought it was a freedom
and it was
like if you are already living in a mousetrap
and someone offers a tiny mousetrap
to go inside you—thank you—

but why my body which I understood increasingly was perfect
had to change so the cishet sex script
which I'd mostly always known was trash
could continue unmodified
was answerable only in terms of a history
I was leaving on a trip with you
half insane I was to be so
into you
I mean you were unaccountably
hot to me in the way that people
sometimes are, our voluptuous
affection a risk, our relationship
volatile because the thread of it went
everywhere, deep into some muscle
out again—
nine months after we broke up
I read a zine by Mira Bellwether
called *Fucking Trans Women*.
It had a diagram of muffing
which is an act that opens space
where none appears to exist
through the power of strategic touch.
And it was not my body in the diagram
but I understood I needed to perform such acts
and have such acts performed on me
that perfection was not a narrow but
an incredibly expansive concept
involving change/refusal
to change/radical change/refusal/
alteration and growth in a loop.

Between getting off the bus and arriving
in the leaf-light on a bed at sunset in our Airbnb
a doctor opened me with a clear plastic

speculum and pulled hard on a thread
while I gasped. It did not hurt very much
though I had been braced for something.
The initial insertion had involved about nine seconds
of the most blinding pain I had ever known
beyond what I had imagined pain could be
the kind of vehicle the rich ride into space
just to see what it's like
I remember I was suddenly so sailing I understood leisure
and that I could become addicted
to the end of pain
the wash of chemicals pain excites, ending
which from the outside looks a lot like
being addicted to pain
though the states are distinct
and as I write this I feel ashamed
the outer marker of my pain threshold
is represented by a tiny T of twisted copper wire
fanning out in me like a margarita umbrella, wishbone
I mean people give birth, for chrissakes
people dilate after vaginoplasty
and even me, if I wanted to tell stories about my body
I am sure I could find a better one
I am thirty-some years old and have lived through
some situations
but pain is a very clarifying state in that
it removes the outside world entirely
you get to focus on your feeling
I was so completely in my feeling
other people were gone
and so was narrative, shame
was a tiny speck down on the ground
it was the perfect lyric moment

the poem my endorphins wrote for the thread
I keep the syllables close
would I repeat them—maybe.
Anyway, the removal took about four seconds
and did not feel like much and
then I got to look at it, my first crush.
It was a plastic T with copper wire coiled
around as I'd been told but hadn't yet witnessed
and then suddenly we were exiting the subway station, late
in comparison to an invisible expectation
our Airbnb host had been holding in his head
though we had not promised him anything
except that we would be unpredictable
for reasons he could not know.
Time is funny, those moments you
re-enter its tense.

He was chilly with an underlying violence.
He was hello in an aggression
I wished to run from but
we'd paid.
I thought about the question of what the fuck
his problem was. It was either
too much power or not enough
and the interesting thing was
I had no way of knowing
unless I asked
and he replied with the truth
which was not a thing I could
imagine happening.
How could I access a mind like Mira Bellwether's
where was the diagram of how to place
my index.
What if he was not the real owner

at all, just some underpaid guy pretending
to own a house in order to comply with a set of rules
someone else was profiting from on the internet
and this charade created complications
I could not know.
Ownership was a lie
we complicated by paying
rent
we were the problem
he could see
we could see
him too
it was important
to look.

The lighting in the rented room was
the kind you should never touch a sunset
was threaded criss-cross like lasers protecting
a work of art we lay down in it
without closing the curtains.
You were afraid to touch me
because of what I'd just been through
I was afraid to be touched
though I was in no pain at all
maybe I was scared not of pain but endorphins
some wires crossed
anyway, I touched you and stayed
partly hidden in my clothes while you opened up
slowly to that amazing, stupefied state
where the minute and the hour and the day
are all the same.

"You have so much
power over me right now I'm gonna
call you Power, Power."

"If you call me that you realize
I will have to call you Glory."
was a dialogue that happened through our bodies
when the veil was thin.
We laughed for longer
than we probably had earned.
Our ignorance of the Lord's Prayer
and the novel by Graham Greene
had not spared us—
there are certain things you can't escape
so just incorporate, wait for the next lover
to take you to a doctor
who will pull the thread.

After you I slept with a very feminine man
I hadn't previously realized I was attracted to
but it turned out I deeply was.
I admit I hoped he was open to trading forms—
that if we fucked in just the right way
I could be a very feminine man
and he could be whatever kind of ambiguous
woman people are constantly mistaking me for.
Of course we never fucked
in just the right way—
I mean we did, it was pure
and endless.

I LOOKED FOR THE EXIT, FOUND A SLEEVE

During the time when everything was going haywire with us
when you were spending days at the hospital with your ex
because her mom was dying suddenly of leukemia
after going to the doctor with a cold
when you were starting a new job that did not love you
because you needed the money
because of a mix-up that after everything
you owed someone
a certain idea of hard embodied
work and you were moving apartments
because the man upstairs would not stop
pacing the entire night and
one morning before you left
a creative energy ran down your arm
and punched your wall
and hurt your hand
and hurt the wall
and knocked on my door pretty hard after
so we could go to the grocery store to get bergamot oil
for your ex's mom's forehead
your ex's forehead
your forehead
(with your thumb at the checkout
you put some roughly on my forehead)
and to tell me what you'd done in your still wild
mood and did you make a hole in it
I assumed you had
I was picturing the plasterboard
fracturing around your slender, sexually
capable wrist and I panicked
you punched your wall, I said
we were passing through a portal in possibility
though you hadn't made a hole

you clarified some weeks later
a small dent
you hurt your hand and
thought some shit was going on with me too
you're going through some shit
you said at several points
on different days
which struck me as manipulative, maybe
but it's only you, love
I said each time, indignantly
you are everyone to me
but I did not say "love"
or explain about the everyone
all those others you umbrella-ed
and we argued in a stairwell
each holding an end
of a giant roll of paper
you'd been making art with.
Your friend, a dancer, would throw himself
against the paper till it tore
completely to shreds
at the climax of his piece
then play dead like he meant it
people watching would cry
a member of the audience
would help him up and play dead too
that was part of it
and for the next show you would unroll him some more.
The roll of paper was 1.5 times the length of the cab
we took it back to your place in
tense and quiet
and there was a giant screen
outside the venue
I want to say forty
but possibly as little as ten feet high

displaying a picture of your friend, his naked
chest because something about
self-destruction that could be
a death spasm
or just emotional frustration
interests people
that confusion
to the extent that we want to see it magnified.

In the haywire time my attention
was called to small things, for example
the moths that had been eating my clothes
for two years, to the point that I did not have much to wear
except polyester blends
which are very ancient
bugs and plants and larger
animals subjected to unimaginable pressure
then woven.
It doesn't breathe I was often sweaty
and it makes sense that at a time like this
you would want to focus
on something you can control
said the therapist I paid for three sessions then abandoned
because she could not have been more wrong.
The moths were like nighttime, forest, sickness
the afterlife, weather—as big and
intricately orchestral
an overwhelming force
as I had known.
I could tantrum or not
it didn't seem to really hurt them
I could use chemicals against us both
are you my real dad
yeah I think so
the delicate masculine

invincible with a lot of tiny wings.

In life there is what you desire
then your impulse.
Then there's what you really desire
and it's all connected.
I wanted to stop losing things
all those scarves and socks my grandmother—
the gorgeous dykey-looking one
Mom's mom
I have always identified with
despite her stated homophobia—
whose stoic quiet drives me
to say words words words in circles
until I've completely surrounded
the truth—had knitted for me.
I wanted there to be a speed limit
the rate at which the moths were eating
the life's work of my grandmother
was enough I felt a nudity
gaining on me
between two people nudity
can be a measure of closeness
can be a symbol for honesty
well, Mormor (that is what I call her
the word in her language
for who she is to me)
are you really a dyke
I imagine myself asking never
or are you more like everyone
a hole in the language I circle
her life's work was returning me
monthly, weekly
to my literal closet
to seek the parts getting eaten

full of apertures through time
which appeared to be accelerating
straight past the ancient question
do I keep my inheritance
or let myself be seen.

I bought a new duvet
made of fossil fuels
a permanent decision
much bigger than me
in space and time
birth control blanket
I regretted immediately
it would never turn threadbare
and clumpy like the old one
it would not nourish any
tiny white caterpillars
if distantly related
to all the huge September plants
the oils they unleashed every day
for your body at the hospital
with your ex because her mom
was dying suddenly.
I admit when I panicked
about the hole I imagined
you left when you moved
it was not for my sake
but for our unborn
unplanned, undiscussed
nonexistent baby who
if the future I was waiting for
were underway
would have needed rescuing
and was I really the kind of person
who could rescue a baby from you

it did not seem very likely.
I mean I am the kind of person who—
you were moving house in a situation
of great emotional distress
and instead of helping you pack or unpack—
I could not seem to get close enough
in the wave pool of you—
I began a ritual whose visuals
resembled moving.
I emptied everything from my dresser drawers and closets.
I went to the laundromat each day carrying
my possessions over one shoulder
in a large golden sack.
I put what had been sterilized in giant Ziplocs
at the centre of the room. I sifted through
imagery. There was a photograph of me in grade seven
looking sad on a campground with a European wiener
that kept confronting me.
I was alone in the picture
not in my sadness
due to penis symbols and the legacy of Europe
obviously
each time it surfaced I thought
this is the tip of something
a privilege
to be on a campground
to have my misery depicted in art
by my family
in a way that returns to me
thanks to possessions, land
that was stolen for me
by the same forces that took my queer childhood
mystery

that's where I come from
this sad sausage fest.

In the intimacy of the haywire
time I gained a sense of responsibility
that kept expanding. I did not know how
to make it stop or if I should.
Usually when I move house
I am only myself, the person moving
rather than everyone, as I was in this case—
the exiting tenant, the entering tenant, you
(who was similarly sitting cross-legged
in a pile of your own shit at this
moment in time when our bodies became photographically
parallel), the dust (which was mostly made of me
I had been living in my apartment long enough)
and of course the moths, which were made of
my dust and clothing and inherited linens
bedding, the hair I had petted off
my landlord's cat, Mimi
because I liked the way she felt.
This state of being everyone—
of inhabiting a world that was a precise reflection
of the ways I had been present or absent
had or had not been expressing my feelings
and grooming, shedding hairs and
invisible flecks of skin, wearing
fabrics made of woven hairs and
invisible plants that once were visible
and growing in dirt outside, in the open air everyone
breathes, of what I had or had not brought inside
kept, shed, forgotten in a drawer
worn again, loved, washed, lost

spilled on, loved again—
naturally made me want to be meticulous.

At some point during the process
of understanding I was everyone
I began to understand the moths
were a ghost, specifically the ghost of a medium-famous
Canadian poet, Al Purdy, at whose house
I had first acquired the infestation.
I had been invited there to do a writing residency.
The poet had been dead for fifteen and a half years
but his stuff was all still there
not all but a lot of it
some had been sold
a lot had been eaten
by moths and I wore
a blue wool sweater almost every day
and worked on poems
and kept the sweater in a drawer
when I remembered
to put it away at night
and kept my body on the bed on the floor
in the light in the kitchen in the morning air
and so the moths that had been nourished on the clothing
furniture, stray hairs, dead skin cells
and literary habits of Al Purdy
began in turn to be nourished by me.

I felt mostly gross
about becoming part of this tradition.
For one thing, I suspected the semi-famous dead
poet, a man of his time
would rather have seen me—wiry, narrow-
titted human stronger than I look—

doing housework than writing poetry.
I can't be a hundred percent sure of this.
I mean he had a couple of women
writer friends. But he also had a wife
and a wife's friend he had a child with.
Into the frames of the photographs on his walls protruded
disembodied arms proffering snacks.
I guess they belonged to someone's wife.
Where to place myself in this picture
was an anxiety that occupied me
throughout my residency.
Could I place myself outside it even
while living in that house.
And what about the land under the house,
the theft of it ongoing. What about everything.
What could I do with my arms
inside or outside a photograph
to give shape to my confused love from here.
Because I could see the poet, how his methods
had failed—even though he had
sometimes spoken against the violences
his house and snacking meant
they were the foundation of his tradition.
And the moths recognized me as part of the tradition
even if the poet himself might not have.
And the moths were the poet, the purest essence of him.
After the body goes, what is left is
dander and lint, these furtive spastic
indirect flutterings that haunt the air at dusk.
I felt myself circling back around to something.

Not since my grandmother's generation
have the women in my family been so oppressed
that they turned the furniture upside down each week

to brush vigorously at the joints, where the legs
meet the base.

It's been a while since any woman
in my bloodline experienced consequences
for failing to air and beat each blanket, cushion, scarf,
sock, mitten, glove, natural lampshade, and rug.
For failing to keep meticulous track
of holiday ornaments, rolls of sewing thread, the interiors
of slippers, felted coaster bottoms, a bloom of dust
behind the baseboard.

There is a mechanism, an anxiety
by which people with some power but not
all the power may project the qualities of their oppressors
onto the beings immediately below, whom they in turn
oppress, this is how an insect can become
a patriarch in the eyes of my white queer
faggy-butch semi-femme
dapple-gendered
medium-powerful position.
I'm not your fucking lady
I tell the moths
who are always quiet
always listening.
Everything I do has an impact
nothing makes anybody go away
not lastingly
the population of my apartment
in terms of ghosts
in terms of energies is pretty stable
everyone always listening
an endless conference
with weapons
to figure something out

I mean a genocidal
war.

Polyester garments are made from bodies
pressed close a long time underground
in their afterlife I was sweating
and the miracle is that even though
the moths can't eat it
they were still well fed
even when all my wool
sweaters were gone there was still so much
they could turn to Swiss cheese
mmmm yes
I learned about what I wore picking it up
out of drawers, putting my finger through
a hole feeling that
small, repetitive emotion
this must have some silk in it, I guess
oh, rayon comes from trees
I didn't know
how natural everything I liked to have
against my body was
had been
the moths knew a lot of things
before me
I watched a powerful video clip once
of a preacher asking people
to stop digging up the dead
by which he meant oil.
Is anyone surprised, he asked
that this would cause spiritual problems
an engine running running running
from its own ghosts
is not a ceremony, it's just—

DON'T YOU FUCK WITH MY ENERGY
is a line from a Princess Nokia song
she screamed it at the show
I was supposed to see with you but saw with someone
else instead, we'd been fighting and
I love that line, how it locates the limit of the self
beyond the apparent edge—
I wanted to scream it too, at you
a week later when I finally peeled my sweaty grey
cotton concert T-shirt off the floor and saw the holes
how the armpits had been ventilated by tiny larval
souls.

Good parenting advice is love yourself
in front of your children, let your children
see you love yourself
because they are you
and in relation to the moths I have to say
I may have screwed up
badly
still I keep trying
as in living in my home
as in raising them
a generation every couple weeks
in hot weather
every six months in cold.

I wiped my walls in poison
went to therapy
we broke up on the phone
and it didn't take—any of it.
Your ex's mom died
across the world my grandmother the closet-
artist had a stroke then was gathered
from her kitchen floor

to hospital
at what may have been the exact instant
some bacteria noticed a hole in my face
and I fell sick with a fever that made me too weak
to keep on fumigating.
I was sweating hard
it was a delicious time for caterpillars
hungry for the condiment of my insight
on the fabric of my surrounds
it turned out to be pneumonia
I had thought it was the weather
(there was a heat wave
thanks to the dead
in the engines of the living)
I collapsed
went to hospital
and you were there for her
I mean me
she who died
I who didn't
you came and held our hands
and time was very layered
as if everything that has happened was happening at once
and it was, I mean it always is.

I wish for you to understand me as a person of expansive
if misdirected empathy, for example
a person had just died, another was facing death
and instead of going to help them—I could not see a way
to help them—I got as near to not breathing as my young
body would take me
you got as near to my hospital bed as you could
without getting back together
until a doctor whose imagination was too small
for us to live in

asked if we were a couple
in order to gauge whether I
could be pregnant—
here I pause to recite
what I could not to him
in the moment: the holy
question of what's in your pants
and mine
(though I wasn't wearing any then—
a man had butterflied
a pair of scissors at the hem, I acted quickly
to prove my consciousness, undid everything)
the question of others, of everyone
elasticity of what it means to fuck
to be together
and basic intelligence we all possess
not just doctors
to squirt fluids into bodies
with implements, anyway—
you said yes, we were together
it was tender
I did not have to pee in any cups
until a few months later when
my illness morphed
your stepmom (sick with cancer
all along in the background)
got suddenly worse
and we broke up on the phone.

The life cycle is a few weeks
in hot weather six months in cold
and at these speeds you can really start
to see the patterns.

I think I fell in love with you

because of the way you helped
my body understand
its relative position.
That night you told me your world story
I fell hard like the dead.
I cannot tell it only repeat
what affected me as a way
to explain something about myself, how
you were a baby, then a kid.
Your grandparents survived genocide.
Your parents survived your grandparents.
If you went to art school
you'd be a dyke, your parents thought
some camouflage—violence
could prevent this
they sent you
to wear dark boots
still a punk still a dyke
still on the wrong side
and now literally
I'd say
not knowing even still
if you'd agree
about the sides
you told me
during the world you mostly peeled potatoes
because your eyes were bad and your heart was
soft and everyone could see.
You did not kill anyone but you saw things.
During the world I mostly ate french fries
on the wrong side, too, of the Atlantic, age sixteen
seventeen, fantasizing about a time
when I could put the life's work
of a body like yours in my mouth for real.

When you hurt one of us you hurt us all
I wrote in my notebook from my bed
in a depressed but clairvoyant mood
thinking of the moment my grandmother hit
the kitchen floor and some bacteria got past
my fear of intimacy because
I don't have enough.

If she really is a dyke or possibly
a faggy or even quite a butch, low-voiced man.
If all her life as it appears from the outside
she has never realized or acted on it.
One time my grandmother, my mom, my sister, and I
were watching *Eternal Sunshine of the Spotless Mind.*
My grandmother stood up and left.
My mom followed.
Later she reported
my grandmother had said
it was because of the gay people.
In that movie there are no gay people
so my mom asked what the gays were doing
that bothered her.
My grandmother's response was bitter
and turned quickly to politicians
with male pattern baldness
who make false promises
(also not depicted in the movie)
leading my mom to believe
she had no idea what gay meant.
I think she knew the word to mean
dishonest and physically
unappealing. And politics
to be everywhere and baldness

as a form of open
secret. The moths especially
like to eat hair.

If she really is about to turn ninety.
If you are not the only
or even the main one hurt
but you are hurt.

A thing about me
is I am terrible with a camera
never think to click it
I have hardly any of you
that aren't at least partial nudes
I have one of a night an insect
flew into your eye and bit it
and half your face swelled up
and mostly it's the only one
I could ever share with people
because we live in a culture
that polices tenderness not
violence, nobody wants to see evidence
I admired your gorgeous bits
everyone is fine to see evidence
your eye was swollen shut
you'd probably rather no one see either
which in the context of my photographic oeuvre
renders you invisible
making me realize the urgency of good art
that makes its own context
I have to get better
at leaving some.

And you—
well, you left.
You had to, I guess.
You just did.
It's possible.
I have learned about leaving
in being left by you
in leaving you
the hole after
is a skill to develop for many purposes on earth
and the healing of the ocean.
You can do it on the phone
I can do it in my
imagination
we can do it together
every day a ceremony
in the parking lot
idling.

When you punched the wall
in the story as I pictured it, you were everyone
who's ever frightened me, which is a lot of people
maybe, fairly or unfairly, everyone I've ever known
but originally my dad, who I feel the need to clarify
was not a puncher to me but used words.
He would get angry about the cat
the position of the salt shaker
in my hands, a few times
he told me to get out of his life
like I was a pestilence and he was God
but it wasn't working.

Also me—
this one time in an argument with my ex

I excused myself to the bathroom
to hit my forehead against the door frame
repeatedly, I do not think I hurt the door frame
I hurt the concept of myself
as an animal in an enclosure
I had entered voluntarily.

When you are everyone and you
leave a place
everyone leaves the place too
because you are everyone—
it's automatically a powerful gesture.

Eventually I listened to my dad's instruction
really heard it
and my heart became more free.

On the other hand, everyone comes with you
when you are everyone it's an endless
intergenerational weapon
conference so in that sense
there is a lot of continuity.

My dad's parents lived through a civil war in which
events happened I do not know the details of—
I know a little
of how my dad's parents
raised him.

When my sister and I were small
he would coach us
to blow tiny spitballs
into the hair of the people in the next booth
at the fast food restaurant.

Once in an argument with my ex I threw a plastic
laundry hamper down the stairs
full of clothes and also as it turns out
my ex's glasses. They were broken
because I chose to break
what I knew in the abstract existed
but did not understand myself
in that moment to be holding.

REUNION

Sometimes personal transformation needs
an agent outside the self
to project the desire to change onto
television makeover shows understand
the self reinventing itself needs to split
into the self + a makeover crew
for the preservation of sense, narrative
through turmoil of becoming
which is probably why
when I got bedbugs right after the moths
and had to empty my closets again
I wondered if this was my version of *Queer Eye*
if all these insects had arrived to make me trans.

SPEECH

Annie Edson Taylor was sixty-three years old
when she became the first person to survive
Niagara Falls in a barrel
and I was six
in the carpeted section of the basement
humping a large brown corduroy
pillow the length of my torso.
It was 1901. Annie had a mattress inside
as cushioning—I could not crawl
inside my pillow, so for safety
wound a skipping rope
around it and my body
arms tucked neatly in, yanking
the end with my teeth to get it tight
this was important.
The river moved swiftly
to the edge of my experience and I
went over and over
understanding perfectly
pleasure and
deadly risk. The falls—
how people had died
and people kept attempting.
I had probably seen a documentary.
People speak of becoming famous
as a process that begins when you are discovered.
Annie was discovered at the bottom of the falls.
I was not. The barrel was Annie's retirement
plan. She thought it would protect her
from poverty, and it is true
when she was in the barrel
she was not in poverty.
She was inside her lived experience.

Later Annie said she would rather stare straight
into a cannon about to blow
than go over the falls that way again
but it is impossible to know if she really meant it
or if she was just saying what you have to say
when you've been discovered—
what power wants to hear. What power wants to hear
is a barrel holds a secret life in a strong current
off a cliff you die the end.
Dying sucked you sure won't
try that again. What power wants to hear
is a barrel holds a secret life in
a strong current, oh no
not the end again, that sucks, try saying it
a few more times, with feeling
power likes repetition
slow repeated motion is the surest
way to push her over the edge.
Meanwhile I keep discovering myself
then talking. I have to
say what I want to hear
when I am found.
I'm becoming more
and more well known.

THE FULL IMPULSE

I have decided instead to do the whole dance in public. To show my body moving through some positions. I am not doing this to overwrite the blank. It's still there, around and between the gestures. It's still infinite and important.

The Spanish Civil War is called the Spanish Civil War because within one country two sides fought and eventually the fascists won and kept power for thirty-nine years. Whereas the Mexican Revolution is called a revolution because when two sides fought, the fascists lost. When Díaz was deposed, dictatorship ended. Frida Kahlo, who was three years old at the time, was born again, a revolutionary and a communist. She often lied about her age to convey this truth—she would say she was born in 1910, the year the revolution started, instead of 1907.

Once I wanted to explain my complicated terrain of stubble and thickets to a lover, and I overshared. I composed an email titled "My body hair: a summary," which contained a list of numbered points. Writing this email was intoxicating, like suddenly unleashing the story of my life. I am still revising and adding to it, even though I sent it a long time ago and that lover has moved on.

Frida Kahlo depicted herself very often in her art. Many of the physical experiences of her life are represented there explicitly.

When I see throw cushions printed with photographs of Frida Kahlo for sale in art gallery gift shops next to paperweights of Vincent van Gogh's *Irises* I think it's unfair that one artist is marketed as a body while the other is marketed as art because, in the same lens that creates this discrepancy, bodies are devalued. And then I remember not to use this lens. When I see rows of Frida Kahlo throw cushions arrayed on a shelf in a store, they appear to me as a kind of army.

A lot of interesting things were happening with gender in the Mexican Revolution. For example, if you read about soldaderas—women soldiers—you will learn that some of them went to the front wearing long skirts, whereas some dressed as men and took male names. Some alternated. And some liked their uniform as a man so much they kept it on for the rest of their lives, thereby troubling this category "women soldiers."

Meanwhile, since there was no socially sanctioned avenue in that war, that I have heard of, for "men soldiers" to wear skirts or contribute to the cause as women, this type of woman soldier stayed hidden in plain sight, I guess, and is not, to my knowledge, written about. Potentially everyone was a woman soldier, or no one. This is true of most wars, as well as most peaceful periods, in most places in modern history.

MY BODY HAIR: A SUMMARY

(1) I got it early, like grade four.

(2) I didn't want it. But I didn't want to remove it either.
What I wanted was continued abstinence from the question.
I pretended it didn't exist.

My Spanish family is not really Spanish but Catalan. The nation of Spain as a whole, and with it my grandmother on my dad's side, was traumatized by the civil war, July 1936 to April 1939. My grandmother was nine when it started and eleven when it ended. Then came the years of dictatorship, during which her language and culture, the names of her eventual children became illegal. For example, my father, named Jordi at birth, in secret, instantly became Jorge in public, by law. A large portion of this story is lost to me, and although I feel it could be my place to bear witness to the contents of the loss, that is not how loss works.

The first time I saw art by Frida Kahlo, I was in high school. My mom took me. The gallery we went to, a forty-five-minute drive downtown, had six or seven of Frida's paintings on loan and some sketches. The paintings were mostly smaller ones. It was the kind of exhibition that makes you think about the smallness of your city in the world. I don't remember having clear feelings about the paintings or Frida. I was watching carefully to remember the details of the art for later, when I would know more. And I was watching other people.

(3) Kids teased me about my hairy pits. Once or twice they even threatened to kill me for them, which feels absurd to report even now. We went to the waterslide park, where I disappeared down long plastic tubes without ever lifting my arms, which was possible. We went to the ocean, where I tried to swim using only forearms, only legs, which was dangerous both socially and physically. When I got home I shut the door to my room and began to snip my armpit hair with a pair of kids' safety scissors. The shorter my hair got, the more deliberate it looked, my hairiness, like a conscious choice, and the more mortifying. I couldn't make it disappear.

The blank begins shortly after my grandmother and her parents baked some money into loaves of bread and dressed up as peasants and fled their home in Barcelona for the mountains. They did this in an effort to hide from both sides: The fascists were opposed to their ethnicity, and the Catalan socialist resistance to their bourgeois status, which abandonment of property did not, by itself, immediately remedy or conceal. There is a story that may or may not be true about them slicing up their palms with knives, to appear as though they had been doing hard labour. In that part of the country at that moment, my grandmother asserted once—memorably, because she almost never spoke about the political situation of her past—you could be killed for having smooth hands. But the cuts, if they existed, were not convincing. My grandmother and her family were recognized as the kind of people who might have money in their loaves, and the loaves were taken.

I think about the impression they must have made, a family of dispossessed rich people trying to get work on farms and blend in with the other labourers and thinking the key to it all was having scabby hands. Imagine the first time someone asked them to do a task, like milking cows or turning compost. There is an angle from which this story of my family's trauma is very funny.

My grandmother was at an age where she probably hated her parents. In this case, so did everyone else. They fled from farm to farm, lying and being discovered, until eventually, for a sustained interval, they disappeared.

I remember a heart and other parts outside the body, in ink or maybe coloured pencil, connected by delicately looping veins. Scissors. An accident, not directly shown but implied repeatedly. Or maybe it was shown and I forgot. (I remember reading somewhere that there is no such thing as forgetting, only repression.) A painting in which Frida's angular face is flanked by leaves and animals. Frida in a men's suit, legs in a V. Then flowers in her hair again.

By the time my dad was six he'd been renamed twice; the third was George. He needed this name to go to school in Canada, where his family had escaped to. It was 1959 or 1960. My dad's third name, though made as an offering to the institutions of the new place, was not particularly accepted by them. His teachers didn't tend to use his given name or speak of him in the singular much at all, preferring to refer to him and his three younger brothers—who, by all accounts, individually or together, were up to no good—as a conglomerate: *the Puigbó boys*. I know this because my dad and his brothers would do the teachers' voices whenever they got together at holidays. "Not another one of the Poooooojbo boys!" they would call out melodically at each other in greeting. Another thing people had called them instead of using their names was *spics*. I don't remember who told me this or why—whether they were trying to explain discrimination in general or teach me not to use slurs or illustrate how successfully we'd assimilated or excuse my dad for having rage problems. No one called my dad or his brothers that word anymore—being white, they had lost their status as "other" with the fading of their accents and the shifting locations of foreign dictatorships and their associated refugees. Anyway, it was a word I thought about.

If spic meant Spanish speaker, then my dad's vulnerability to the slur as a child was ironic because, although he and his family could speak Spanish and had at various points been compelled to perform that culture, one could just as easily say that they were running from the Spanish—from those political elements that, after the war, came to occupy that label—as one could say that they were Spanish. They spoke Catalan at home, and this was also most likely the language that my dad would get whacked across the palm or the butt for in school when he spoke it to himself or his brothers on the playground. The world must be full of these kinds of ironies, I thought, confusions of relationship with identity. And maybe there is even some truth in that confusion—like if you have been hurt at close enough range by someone or some group, you might carry an element of them with you, so that, perceived from certain angles, at sufficient distance, you and your oppressor appear so entangled as to be indistinguishable.

(4) Around seventh grade I started surreptitiously shaving. Shaving would have been allowed if I'd asked—I could have had my own razor and a lesson—but speech on this topic was completely beyond me, so instead I buzzed myself haphazardly with my mom's electric razor from the seventies whenever the house was empty. I'd wait for the sound of the car pulling out and then I'd be like, action stations. It was like simultaneously being a farmer tasked with shearing an untamed animal and the animal itself. The plan, the equipment, the morning, the element of surprise, limbs everywhere, nicks, adrenaline.

I don't speak to my dad anymore. He was an unpredictable parent, verbally and emotionally abusive, and generally on a hair trigger about the fact that I was alive and not always completely controllable. I mentioned the salt shaker earlier. For some reason that incident seems emblematic. I was about twelve and picked up the salt shaker at the dinner table and he just completely lost his shit because it was *his* salt shaker, and he didn't like the way I was holding it. There were a lot of moments like this—an airhorn I'd never touched but was blamed for breaking, dirty dishwater I emptied but should not have. He couldn't handle when I showed kindness to animals. There was a thing he would say to me sometimes after raging at me, that no one would ever love me unless I changed my ways. I think this is because he knew—right from the beginning, long before I did—that I was queer. I don't know how he knew—it was the same kind of knowing the mean kids had in school. Conversely, I don't know how everyone else didn't know—I think they must have known, then suppressed the information out of compassion.

The way I came out to my dad was he called me from across the country when I was twenty-three. He hardly ever called me. I had just returned to my apartment from my lover's place. How on earth could he know where I had been, to time his call like this. Was it possible he had died and become an omnipresent ghost, or was it just that all people are visible if you decide to look? "So are you one of those too," he asked—but really just stated. I felt him staring straight at me through the receiver. "Yeah," I replied. "I am."

"One of those" referred to my dad's brother, who had come out to the family as bisexual a few weeks earlier, after testing positive for HIV. At the time I was the only person in my family who—being in contact with the kind of queers who knew these things—had heard of the advances in antiretroviral drugs that enabled many people with that diagnosis to live. Other family members seemed to expect my uncle's coming out would lead to his immediate death, like in the movies. I was not close to that uncle, but I felt his revelation as a beginning. "You are lucky," my dad continued. "If I had known that anyone around me was bisexual ten or even two or three years ago…" and I knew that through a certain lens—in which the field of all possible luck has been shrunk to a question of death: now or later, and violence: from your family or from somewhere else—I *was* lucky. At a certain point, I said goodbye and hung up. From that point on, my dad's rages, which could only happen at long intervals because I lived far away and hardly ever spoke to him, began to include the line, "Get out of my life. Get out of my life and leave me alone." The second or third or fifth time he demanded this—had he always been demanding this?—when I was thirty-two and had flown home, fearful and conflicted, to wish him well as he recovered from an emergency heart surgery (or, more honestly, to see what it was I felt for him, what his survival might mean in relation to my own), I took him at his word.

My dad has distinctive eyebrows. They are thick and dark, white by now, I guess, and level, like two facing caterpillars. I have inherited them sort of, in the sense that if you were to look at us standing side by side you would see the narrative thread, though my eyebrows are less full and more curved. Once, a couple of years after we stopped speaking for the second or third or fifth time, the one that stuck, I had the unsettling experience of walking into a coffee shop called the Barcelona Café, a name I had assumed was purely decorative, on my dad's name day, April 23, a date that had been unknown to me. (When my dad was growing up, birthdays were unimportant, but saints' name days were observed, whereas when I was growing up we ignored my dad's name day in favour of his birthday.) His name, the original one, was written festively in huge lettering on a chalkboard beside the espresso list. Seated at a large table to the left of the counter were six or seven men about his age, with his same narrow build, speaking Catalan and playing chess. They all had his eyebrows. I didn't go back there, and a year or two later, the café closed, leaving the memory of the incident unanchored, like a dream.

As a teenager I worried substantially about eyebrows. As I wrote in the document that began as an email to my lover and unfurled into the story of my life:

(5) In high school I had this idea that I had a unibrow—I didn't, but perception is interesting. My religion was that it was strong and dark and qualified me for social ostracism unless I plucked it. I would begin the task facing the bathroom mirror. But each time I brought the tweezers close, there was an irrepressible opposing impulse not to pluck. I could never manage more than a couple of hairs (there was hair there, just not as thick as I thought—a layer of fuzz not visible from any distance). I had one goal: pluck my unibrow! For real this time! I kept deferring it. Each time I failed to fully pluck my imaginary unibrow I felt that my existence in the world outside the bathroom was threatened, and deservedly so. Why was I so useless?

Around this time, I bought myself a razor and nonchalantly put it in the shower. Nobody ever mentioned it or asked about it, and I never brought up the subject either. At this point I was shaving legs, armpits, edges of pubic hair (but not, like, the meat of it), belly, nipples.

I came out as trans in 2018, when I was thirty-four. I renamed myself a year later, and began taking testosterone a couple of years after that. This new self-understanding—that I was not a man or a woman but something else, something sort of man-adjacent and at the same time extremely fruity, a person who desired a five o'clock shadow and a closet full of leotards—threw a lot of things into question, among them my teenage relationship with how I looked. A lot of the things I'd thought I hated about myself—"mannish" face, habit of walking bouncily with long strides, perceptible body hair—turned out to be assets in the project of making myself legible as "not a woman." Suddenly these qualities felt euphoric.

Maybe the reason I had never been very effective at plucking my eyebrows or admitting to anyone that I shaved was that I was reluctant to perform rituals I associated with girls and women. Maybe the reason I thought my hair-removal failures made me unworthy of existing was that the world told me trans and gender-nonconforming people didn't deserve to exist. Maybe my fear of having a unibrow was a fear of something else—of looking like my dad or another man in my ancestry? Of transgressing gender norms like those images I'd seen of Frida Kahlo?—and at bottom it wasn't a fear at all but a desire.

I am thinking now about self-image. In 2013, the Dove soap company released a video called *Dove Real Beauty Sketches* as part of an ad campaign. The video documents an experiment in which conventionally beautiful women of several races and ethnicities sit behind a curtain and, one at a time, describe themselves to a forensic sketch artist on the other side. Not being able to see the women, the artist makes portraits of them based solely on their self-descriptions. Then the artist makes a second series of portraits of the same women as described by strangers who have met them once. The portraits are paired and hung in a gallery, revealing a substantial gulf between how the women see themselves and how they are seen by others. The women have universally described themselves as "uglier"—smaller eyes, squarer jaws, fatter cheeks, larger noses, deeper wrinkles, etc.—than they are in the descriptions of strangers and in real life as the camera shows it. They look older, heavier, more masculine and melancholy than as seen through the videographer's lens. A more diverse array of body types and features exists in this personally imagined realm than in reality according to the ad. The tag line of the ad, "You're more beautiful than you think," suggests that these ugly portraits are a hallucination, a baseless anxiety. Nobody actually looks like that. And of course, that's a lie. The soap company took deliberate steps not to cast the people who look like that.

When I think about this commercial, I think about time, about family and community, and I think about transition. That's who the ugly versions represent to me—future selves, relatives, ancestors, childhood friends, people the subjects might have passed in the street and remembered for some reason, othergendered selves.

Maybe the women in the commercial don't know how to be in relationship to these people, and that's why they make them anxious. Or maybe the anxiety is something the soap company invented and not actually what the women feel. If anything, it's being confronted with the "beautiful," "real" versions of themselves that seems to make the women anxious. I like to think about the participants in the commercial delivering their ugly self-descriptions as part of an organized rebellion against capitalism's erasure of so many people. Subconscious or deliberate—it doesn't really matter. The rebellion has achieved a small victory. First the ugly versions took over an art gallery. Then they got on television.

The mainstream narrative of trans identity, the one I grew up with and still encounter regularly, is that transgender people are sick in the head and aren't living in reality. Over and over, implicitly and explicitly, we are told we are hallucinating our genders and that we would be better off—and much better-looking—if we could just get back to conforming with what we were assigned to be. When I was finally able to validate the "ugly version" of myself as not merely an anxious hallucination or a myth, but the edge of something, a genuine desire for how I wanted to be seen, something revolutionary happened.

Desiring to look a certain way is fraught and complicated—I don't mean to suggest that it isn't. Systems of looking are messed up to begin with, and imagination isn't some special outside place free of all the garbage dynamics and premises that govern the rest of the world. It's not a magic ticket to becoming free, or a place where no one can get hurt or cause harm or be held responsible for what comes up. I mean only that what's imagined—or what we've been told to write off as imaginary—is often real.

My grandmother usually seemed like she was elsewhere. She would gaze off into a part of the room where no people were and keep talking. Often the subject was herself, how hot she used to be in her twenties, with descriptions of her legs and how she looked in a swimsuit, and while at the time I found this embarrassing, in retrospect I am impressed. She never ate or served a vegetable without boiling the absolute snot out of it first, to guard against the kinds of illness that happen without refrigeration, even though she had refrigeration. Her vocabulary in English was eccentric. My favourite of her expressions was rhododendrons instead of rodents, as in, "I've been having a problem with rhododendrons in the basement"—I think she thought it was the fancier, full-length version of the term. As a kid I had pet gerbils, then a mouse, and for a while I had the idea that "veteran" was the short form of "veterinarian," which is what I wanted to be when I grew up. I was confused by the way adults would fall silent when I told them about my desired profession. By combining my vocabulary with my grandmother's I could say that I wanted to be a veteran for rhododendrons, or that people should take their rhododendrons to veterans when hurt or sick, and, even though this makes no sense, I feel like it means something, that this is how people talk on the plane where my grandmother and I understand each other.

(6) Three days after I went to university, I fell in love. She didn't shave, and she didn't eat meat. Suddenly I didn't either. My love was the repressed kind, that I didn't admit existed even as I shaped and manipulated it—the same approach I had taken with my hair, though now I tried openly to love my hair, as if rehearsing for openly loving this woman who was "only" my friend. It wasn't easy.

My grandmother was resolutely devoted to the Catholic church, and exactly as homophobic as the priests there encouraged. She would get involved in campaigns to roll back gay rights or prevent new laws from going through. This involved bringing home large parcels of leaflets with bold-font proclamations about how gay people were going to burn in hell eternally, and deserved to, and handing these around the neighbourhood. Times New Roman on a pale blue background embellished with pictures of Jesus and rays of light. I remember being at lunch with my mom and my grandmother in late high school. My grandmother handed my mom a stack of leaflets, to "share with the neighbours." I expected my mom to decline, but instead she smiled politely and put the fat pile in her purse. This was in the interval before I had admitted to myself that I was queer but was nevertheless paying meticulous attention to my surroundings, to see how the sides would form when my information surfaced. Later I argued with my mom forcefully about gay rights in the abstract. She agreed, but said it was better not to confront my grandmother. Besides, no gay people had been present, so none had been hurt. She put the pamphlets in the recycling bin, in our open carport, and on collection day wind strewed them up and down the block.

I didn't want to force a confrontation either. Sometimes I think about how long I really waited to make my position known, how difficult an interval it is to measure. Do I know my position yet? At nineteen I conceded in an argument with my boyfriend, who kept breaking up with me to come out as gay, that I was queer or something too, and pretty soon after told my friends. Shortly after my dad called me and confronted me in my early twenties about being "one of those," I called my mom to let her know I was bisexual. I had to let her know again a few years later when I ended a long relationship with a man (in her eyes I'd been reset to straight). At thirty-four I told everyone I was trans, and at thirty-five I changed my name, but I was thirty-seven before the change was legal and I could be addressed by that name if, for example, I went to a clinic or a hospital or enrolled in a course. Up until that point it was a constant argument. If I were going to tell a lie about my age in the mode of Frida Kahlo I could say the time I spent living under a name that misgendered me was the length of the dictatorship in Spain, thirty-nine years, though in reality it was only thirty-eight.

My grandmother died on my birthday. That's not a lie, just a fact that resembles a metaphor. At the extremely Catholic funeral, the priest confused my grandmother's name with mine, and delivered my eulogy until someone, a church friend of my grandmother's, called out loudly, interrupting him. When years later, after changing my name, I began to refer to my old name as my "deadname," I thought about this, how my old name had already had a funeral a long time ago that coincided with the death of my grandmother.

Names are a negotiation with power, always. Renaming myself and having to argue to get people to address me as the new word confronted me with this fact. If you get to call yourself, out loud, a name that matches how you see yourself, that's a privilege. If what you call yourself and what others call you matches—and it's not because you conceded to or reclaimed their language—that's a privilege too.

I looked up the history of *spic*. It doesn't come from *Hispanic* like I assumed. It may be a variant pronunciation of the word "speak." This theory is based on an account of Panamanians in the early 1900s addressing American labourers (who had been sent to dig the Panama Canal) with the phrase "Speak English," to express that they could communicate in that language, or were willing to try. The Americans then turned the Panamanians' pronunciation back on them as a derogatory label. If this is the origin of the slur, then it names not ethnicity or even language but effort—someone who is making an attempt to perform within the conventions of a colonizing culture and whose effort and process are palpable.

This feeling of a word, a source of pain opening up under the slightest bit of pressure and revealing itself to be connected to everything I thought it was connected to but differently, or the feeling of things continuing beyond the edge of my awareness, that there's a much bigger way of making sense perpetually just out of reach—or maybe I can reach it after all, if I track all of the connections, the points the narrative fails—is the feeling of being alive, I guess. When I was reading about Frida Kahlo, I learned, for example, that there was a point at which she and her husband Diego were fundraising to send supplies to the Republican troops in Spain. And so it's possible, even if not very likely, that a weapon or a can opener or a tin of fish touched or at least purchased by Frida Kahlo later touched or was observed in use by my grandmother, and what would that have been like? Could either one of them have grasped or intended the full meaning of the exchange? Mexico was one of the few countries willing to openly support the socialist side in Spain—Frida's fundraising was part of a larger, coordinated, government-backed effort—and this was thanks, of course, to the revolution that had started twenty-six years before. So the way I spoke earlier about the Mexican Revolution and the Spanish Civil War as separate events with opposite results isn't accurate—the civil war in this sense was just a chapter in the revolution, or the revolution (which even within Mexico was extremely long and chaotic—a Wikipedia list of factions in the war names not two, but thirteen sides; some are pursuing their aims to this day) was continuing as a civil war.

(7) I flip-flopped, tried to camouflage. I shaved to have sex with men and with women who shaved. I grew my hair out to have sex with women who didn't shave. When, for a few months after finishing my undergrad, I worked on farms in the mountains outside Barcelona (I was curious to see where my family was from—my dad had never been back) I grew everything out lush to match the other hippies, but between farms, passing through the city, I'd feel immediately gross and shave it all off. Once my razor got too clotted with hair after shaving one of my legs to continue with the other. I spent maybe two weeks in this state of having one leg that was hairy and another that was catching up.

Improbably, though my grandmother and her family lost everything in the war, they emerged on the far side of it in possession of a pair of severely tarnished, thinly silver-plated candelabras, one of which I inherited. I do not know very much about my candelabra except that whatever precious metal was once on it is mostly gone now, and it is decorated like a Roman banquet table, with clusters of grapes in relief. It's a thing I kept because I felt like I had to, moving it between apartments, in with a lover, out again, never knowing quite where to place it among my things. There wasn't any good place for an object like this, either in my physical reality or in the narratives I had received. Why would people pretending to be peasants, carrying all of their worldly goods in a wooden cart and so afraid of being found out that they roughed up their hands with knives, assume the risk and inconvenience of travelling with a set of silver-plated centrepieces? And how, through successive flights from farm to farm, packing up each time they were discovered, did they manage to keep the candelabras with them?

The inexplicability of the candelabra aggravated me. It seemed a failure—whether of ethics, narrative, logic, or all three, I could not decide. It opened the door to further questions about the story of my family's fleeing, like why bake money into loaves of bread at a time when (I have read) there was a bread shortage, when people, kids in hospitals among others, were starving, and currency was increasingly without practical value? Wouldn't it have been smarter in this time and place, if you had only those two materials to work with, to hide bread in sacks full of money?

I tried to picture the size and shape of the loaf that contained my candelabra. An enormous disc with a silver stem? A triangle? When I first moved into my current apartment, a place without much closet space, the problem of where to store the candelabra became acute. In the end I placed it prominently on top of a cabinet and made a handwritten sign, which I tacked to the wall just above: Some Difficult Light Sources I Inherited. There were two arrows on the sign. One pointed to the candelabra, the other to a pretty French oil lamp my dad had given me as a present once, which I also didn't know what to do with. I remember hoping that contextualizing these painful objects with language would help me live with them more openly. I did notice it was odd that I no longer had any relationship with the people who had given me these objects, and yet the objects continued to travel with me. Another irony was that while the progression from candelabra to oil lamp represented an evolution in lighting technology, the essential problem (how to be loved) remained unchanged. I thought that maybe these lamps were like my body. I had inherited my body. I could not exchange it. Maybe, just as it was my task to let my body shine in this world regardless of its origins, I should let the candelabra and the oil lamp shine too. It was terrifying to light them. Like waking up ghosts.

If the story of my grandmother's family fleeing were made into a movie—genre uncertain—there would be a scene in which recently landowning people now pretending to be peasants, travelling with a wooden cart full of oddly shaped loaves with bits of silver protruding here and there, encountered a hungry soldier tasked with checking people's palms for callouses during a bread shortage.

I imagine this soldier—gender uncertain, armed with Frida Kahlo's gun—picking up the loaf that contained my candelabra by the stem, like a drumstick, and beginning to take hungry bites.

And when that soldier finished and handed you back the tarnished bone to carry through the rest of the war...were you ashamed? Is that why you carried it?

Were the candelabras difficult light sources you inherited?

(8) In my early twenties, I got mysteriously sick. I had a lot of weird symptoms that seemed unrelated but were happening all at once—sinus infections, weight loss, heart palpitations, fatigue, thirst. Doctors couldn't figure it out, which made them ashamed I guess, so they tried to shame me too. A doctor asked, apropos of nothing, how many sex partners I'd had in the past year and, when I told him, said that I could

expect "health problems" unless I cut back. Another doctor, an endocrinologist, saw the fine, dark hairs growing in a line down from my belly button and noted them as abnormal, perhaps a symptom of my condition. That's a lot of hair, she remarked. I started shaving them.

When I was fourteen, my friend, who was fifteen, lost her earring in shag carpet. We searched on hands and knees until our faces came close. I had an impulse, unpremeditated, to lunge forward and put my lips on hers, which I almost did. It was terrifying how close I came to risking everything. The shag carpet was green and endless. I remember the way it felt between my panicked fingers. My friend was looking for her earring, which she never found. I was looking for a pretext, which found me first and then I ran from it. We stayed in that landscape for years. The first time I kissed a woman I was eighteen and denied any sexual intent—we were just being "friendly." Three months later, when she said she had feelings for me I told her I loved her too but wasn't queer. She knew I was lying. I believed in my lie so fully I was innocent. We stayed in this strange sort of impasse, kissing drunkenly up against walls when we got the chance. The first time I kissed a woman with intent I was twenty-two and drunk on a bottle of homemade fruit wine with outrageous alcohol content my dad had given me shortly after my grandmother's funeral. In my grandmother's home there was green shag carpeting too, wall to wall, concealing who knows how many lost objects. The first woman I kissed with intent had a hard-to-find clit, or I was just that inexperienced. I remember having to reach for it under the shelf of her pubic bone, so much lower than I'd thought, hidden under hair. I am not going to say it was like a pearl. I am not going to say it belonged on my high school friend's ear. There was this sense of the landscape ending.

I dated gay men too. Their friends didn't like me—there was this joke that I was working for the Christian right. I dated several people who have since come out as trans. When I think back on times I dated gay men or straight women I wonder if it was me or them who broke the promise on the label.

The day I gave my candelabra to the people was unremarkable except for the fact that I had realized I could. I took it to the thrift store a ten-minute walk down the road, along with some shirts I didn't like anymore and some Mason jars I wasn't using and a container of lamp oil I had bought back when I thought the solution to my pained emotions about my dad's pretty oil lamp was to keep lighting it. (I had already given away the oil lamp.) The people had done nothing to deserve the candelabra, which was simultaneously a priceless historical artifact, evidence, a heavy burden, and a decoration in medium-questionable taste (the grapes!) likely to fetch a maximum of four to five dollars, the after-overhead fraction of which would be donated to a shelter for women experiencing violence. (How the shelter defined "women" and "violence" was something I did not know, and I hoped that if they were the kind of place that would tell people their bodies or experiences didn't register, my candelabra would haunt them from fiscal year to fiscal year until they understood something.) I had done nothing to deserve my candelabra either. I left it in a white box with a lid at the entrance of the thrift store and went home and eventually made some dinner. While I cooked, I fantasized about calling the shelter to discuss the case of someone like me in the event of a sudden loss of safety. In the fantasy, I was extremely convincing—they agreed to drop the word "women" from their name and put trans people in positions of leadership, and when the violence broke out I moved in along with all kinds of gender-marginalized people and none of us were gendered from the outside any longer. My candelabra sold for a million dollars at auction, and we bought nice furniture for our house.

When I think of revolution, I imagine it as a series of small, courageous, flawed attempts to risk everything.

Where can you go, a new acquaintance asked me, to be your full impulse? We were waiting for a bus together, and as they said this they were kicking the bus-stop pole lightly. They were on their way to a concert that was going to be a quiet concert; they worried their current energy would be too much for the room, hence the question. I didn't know where I could go, and that was unsettling. How had I missed asking myself this question earlier. There were two questions: the nature of the impulse, the location of the venue that would hold it. They said they thought they could be their full impulse in a contact improvisation dance session with strangers. "No—" they corrected after a moment, "after, when I am having sex with one of the people I met improvisationally dancing. That is probably my full impulse." I admired them for knowing this.

I am thinking about choices. Scenario 1: you join the revolutionary army as a ticket to being seen as a man. Scenario 2: you consent to be seen as a man or "mannish" as a ticket to participate in the revolution. Scenario 3: you have no particular desire to be seen as a man or be a revolutionary, but you were born or kidnapped or otherwise coerced into it—you have no other safe option.

If the venues of masculinity and the revolution were unticketed, masculinity could be peaceful and the revolution could be feminine. If masculinity were not an army, no one would be punished for deserting, and if femininity were not a punishment, the arms could be instruments of pleasure. I would like to elaborate these states because I suspect they are my venue—the dirt in which something very *me*, very *I* could go shooting up and blooming down, but it is hard to find the words, let alone speak them. The venue is a blank, language becomes a blank, whole sections of my body and its desires are revealed as blank. A blank is a densely packed field of information you don't know how to be in relationship to.

NOTES

This book is a work of memory and imagination. People, animals, places, and situations have been, to varying degrees, fictionalized. Some people mentioned in the text are amalgams of several real people; some events are stand-ins for other events; most names have been changed.

Some Animals and Their Housing Situations
The list of extinctions and declines in species populations is for the year 2014 and was taken from a blog post written by Dr. David A. Steen on the site Living Alongside Wildlife, accessed in early 2015: https://livingalongsidewildlife.com/?p=2478.

Six Boxes
When I wrote the list of violent acts that appears at the beginning of the piece, I anonymized the stories to prevent survivors from being identified. I recombined, stripped out, or, in some cases, altered details. I took care to convey an accurate sense of weight/situational entrapment with each incident, but the experiences I've described should not be assumed to belong to any specific person or to have happened exactly as written.

The Ariana Reines quote "writing can be more than good" comes from the essay "Sucking" published in *Action Yes* issue 6 (2007): http://www.actionyes.org/issue6/reines/reines-sucking.html.

Mirror
This piece describes a dance choreographed and performed by Hanako Hoshimi-Caines in Montreal in 2019. I was invited by Hoshimi-Caines and the Fondation Jean-Pierre Perreault to be part of a group of artists and writers documenting the dance, which was intended to be recorded exclusively by these notes and drawings. My description has been reworked for this collection.

I Looked for the Exit, Found a Sleeve
The line "Don't you fuck with my energy" is from the song "Brujas" by Princess Nokia, on the album *1992 Deluxe*.

The Full Impulse
The details of the story about my grandmother's family fleeing through the mountains in Spain during the civil war, as well as their economic situation before the war, are based on things told to me (or that I overheard) as a child, which were in turn based on my grandmother's understanding of a situation she lived through as a child. I have not been in a position to clarify or verify any of these details as an adult.

The email I sent about my body hair (of which the numbered points represent a revised excerpt) was part of a correspondence on this topic; my correspondent at one point sent me a link to Paniz Khosroshahy's essay "Not Shaving Isn't Always a Choice for Women of Colour" published in gal-dem in 2016 (https://gal-dem.com/shavi ngforwoc/?fbclid=IwAR3LhQGwXt-J2VWSMSl7wSkfvFgEoWL7x9 9yrNyDq4gHR4NwYMkkngN4VHI). Among other things, the essay addresses the fact that women of colour generally face steeper social penalties for not shaving than white women and can wind up in an impossible bind in so-called "progressive" spaces where not shaving is coded as liberation. I reference it here as a necessary counterpoint to a piece in which I speak about my relationship to my body hair as a white person socialized to be a girl, and in which the growing of my hair could be read as liberatory. While Khosroshahy's essay gives a cis woman's perspective, racialized trans/two-spirit/gender variant experiences of body hair and hair removal are also necessary to consider.

The account I give of the etymology of the slur *spic* is based on the article "Spic-O-Rama: Where 'Spic' Comes From, and Where It's Going" by Juan Vidal, published on NPR's blog Code Switch:

https://www.npr.org/sections/codeswitch/2015/03/03/388705810/
spic-o-rama-where-spic-comes-from-and-where-its-going.

The line "My candelabra sold for a million dollars at auction and we
bought nice furniture for our house" references the Barenaked Ladies
song "If I Had a Million Dollars." The members of the Barenaked
Ladies—to my knowledge, all cis men—at one point posed naked,
with penises tucked, for a photograph I remember seeing in the
newspaper as a child and which can still be found online (e.g.,
https://www.nme.com/blogs/nme-blogs/stars-of-album-covers-as-
they-look-today-761548). Seeing that image again today, I am struck
that they look transmasculine.

Texts that informed my understanding of Frida Kahlo's life and art
include:

Fuentes, Carlos, and Sarah M. Lowe. *The Diary of Frida Kahlo:
An Intimate Self-Portrait*. New York: Abrams, 2005.

Herrera, Hayden. *Frida: A Biography of Frida Kahlo*. New
York: Harper & Row, 1983.

Beyond basic online searches, my understanding of soldaderas and
their role in the Mexican Revolution is based on the following books
and articles:

Arrizón, Alicia. "Soldaderas and the Staging of the Mexican
Revolution," *The Drama Review* 42, no. 1 (Spring 1998):
90–112.

Poniatowska, Elena, and David Dorado Romo. *Las Soldaderas:
Women of the Mexican Revolution*. El Paso: Cinco Puntos
Press, 2006.

Salas, Elizabeth. "Soldaderas: New Questions, New Sources," *Women's Studies Quarterly* 23, no. 3/4 (1995): 112–116.

Other texts I consulted about the Mexican Revolution more generally include:

Joseph, Gilbert M., and Jürgen Buchenau. *Mexico's Once and Future Revolution: Social Upheaval and the Challenge of Rule since the Late Nineteenth Century.* Durham, NC: Duke University Press, 2013.

Legrás, Horacio. *Culture and Revolution: Violence, Memory, and the Making of Modern Mexico.* Austin: University of Texas Press, 2017.

Wasserman, Mark. *The Mexican Revolution: A Brief History with Documents.* Boston: Bedford/St. Martin's: 2012.

Texts that informed my understanding of the Spanish Civil War include:

Gellhorn, Martha. "The War in Spain" (1936); repr. in *The Face of War*. New York: Simon and Schuster, 1959, 9–41.

Graham, Helen. *The Spanish Civil War: A Very Short Introduction.* New York: Oxford University Press, 2005.

Orwell, George. *Homage to Catalonia.* London: Secker & Warburg, 1938; repr. London: Penguin Classics, 2013.

ACKNOWLEDGMENTS

The works in this manuscript were composed over a long period of time, beginning in 2014, during which I had intermittent support from the Canada Council for the Arts, the Ontario Arts Council, and the Conseil des arts et lettres du Québec. In 2015, I benefited from a two-month funded residency at the Al Purdy A-Frame, on the traditional lands of the Haudenosaunee, Huron-Wendat, and Anishinaabe peoples. Most of the rest of the work took place in Tio'tia:ke (Montreal), on unceded Kanien'kehá:ka land that is also, historically and ongoingly, a meeting place for other nations, including Algonquin-Anishinaabe, Atikamekw, and Huron-Wendat people. In recognition of the debt my writing practice owes—materially and intellectually—to Indigenous land and knowledge (to question gender or the violence of the colonizing cultures I was born into relies, by definition, on ideas nurtured within Indigenous cultural lineages), I pay a regular portion of my income as reparations to individuals and to organizations of land defenders. I believe all land should be returned to Indigenous stewardship and that systemic reparations at the state level are necessary beyond individual efforts, and I do my best to advocate for these changes. I am grateful beyond measure for my relationship with the lands I have lived on and for the daily opportunity to move toward repair.

An early version "Self Love" was published in the *Toronto Review of Books*; early versions of "Some Animals and Their Housing Situations" were published in *Monkey Business* and as an e-chapbook by The Elephants press; "Reason" was first published in *The Elephants* journal; an early version of "Six Boxes" was published in *The Capilano Review* and subsequently anthologized in *Best Canadian Essays 2019*; an early version of "Mirror" was published as part of a zine made by the Fondation Jean-Pierre Perreault in 2020; an early version of "I Looked for the Exit, Found a Sleeve" was published as a limited-edition handmade chapbook by Skyebound Press and used as a score for flamenco dance by Katherine McLeod; "Speech" was first published in *The Malahat Review* and subsequently won the PK Page Founders' Award for Poetry. Thank you to the editors and judges.

My gratitude to the readers who gave me feedback on early drafts and later ones—among them Naya Valdellon, Erin Robinsong, Fazeela Jiwa, Nadia Chaney, David Bradford, Michael Nardone, and Rebecca La Marre. Thank you to Itzel Daniela, Bianca Rae Messinger, Anahita Jamali Rad, Riley Jay, and Robin Simpson for the influence of their friendship and conversation on this text (and, in Robin's case, for letting me borrow his library card so many times). I'm especially grateful to have been able to work with Mattilda Bernstein Sycamore as a substantive editor, whose careful thinking, queer ideas, and brilliant sense of prose rhythm have made this a better book; in a similar vein, I'm indebted to H. Felix Chau Bradley for their insightful line edits, to Shannon Whibbs for her sensitive copy edits, and to Charlene Chow for her careful proofreading. To all who gave me feedback on the writing in this book, I am grateful for your insights; any lingering failures in the text are my own. Thank you to Tree Abraham for designing such a gorgeous cover and to everyone at Book*hug Press for taking a chance on this project and supporting it.

ABOUT THE AUTHOR

©Justine Latour

River Halen is an award-winning writer of Catalan and Danish descent living in Tio'tia:ke (Montreal). Their poems and essays dealing with relation, ecology, transformation, and sexuality have been published widely in Canada, as well as in the U.S., Australia, and in translation in Japan. Their work has been shortlisted for the Trillium Book Award for Poetry and a National Magazine award, and selected for inclusion in *Best Canadian Essays* as well as *Best Canadian Poetry*. Halen is currently working on a book about joy and a research project about alternative ways (beyond the physical) of asserting and perceiving gender.

ABOUT THE ESSAIS SERIES

Drawing on the Old and Middle French definitions of *essai*, meaning first "trial" and then "attempt," and from which the English word "essay" emerges, the works in the Essais Series challenge traditional forms and styles of cultural enquiry. The Essais Series is committed to publishing works concerned with justice, equity, and diversity. It supports texts that draw on seemingly intractable questions, to ask them anew and to elaborate these questions. The books in the Essais Series are forms of vital generosity; they invite attention to a necessary reconsideration of culture, society, politics, and experience.

For more information visit bookhugpress.ca/product-category/essais-series/

COLOPHON

Manufactured as the first edition of
Dream Rooms
in the fall of 2022 by Book*hug Press

Edited for the press by Mattilda B. Sycamore
Copy edited by Shannon Whibbs
Proofread by Charlene Chow
Type + design by Tree Abraham

Printed in Canada

bookhugpress.ca